Llamas and Alpacas

A Guide to Management

Gina Bromage

THE CROWOOD PRESS

First published in 2006 by
The Crowood Press Ltd
Ramsbury, Marlborough
Wiltshire SN8 2HR

www.crowood.com

This impression 2009

British Library Cataloguing-in-Publication Data
A catalogue record for this book is available from the British Library.

ISBN 978 1 86126 884 6

All photographs by the author except where stated otherwise.
Line-drawings by Keith Field.

Edited and designed by
OutHouse!
Shalbourne, Marlborough
Wiltshire SN8 3QJ

Printed and bound in Singapore by Craft Print International Ltd

Contents

Acknowledgements

There are many people without whom this book could not have been written, and I am deeply indebted to those who have provided photographs, as well as other kinds of support. My mother, Val Ridgway, who is responsible for my interest in camelids, and who has funded a great deal of my learning, deserves much gratitude in particular. Chris Eke and Jo Harwood of UK Llamas have been a great source of encouragement and a great deal of practical help; they have my particular thanks, as does John Gaye who has written the chapter on the marketing of fleece. Thanks are also due to Yocom-McColl Testing Laboratories, Inc. for granting permission to publish one of their Testing Laboratories histogram reports. Other members of the BVCS and the South West Alpaca Group, too numerous to mention individually, have variously and generously contributed with experiences, information and images. My own knowledge has been built on foundations laid by, amongst others and in no particular order, Murray Fowler, Eric Hoffman, John Mallon, Chris Cebra, David Anderson, David Pugh, Marty McGee, Clare Hoffman, Gail Birutta, Walter Bravo, Ahmed Tibary, Jane Vaughan, and Amanda Van den Bosch.

Preface

From a chance encounter with alpacas in early 1999, my close involvement with camelids became inevitable after I showed them to my mother at the Royal Bath and West Show of the same year. She immediately resolved to buy some alpacas when she retired to the West Country a few months later and, as her default veterinarian, my fate was sealed. In those days very few of my colleagues had any camelid expertise, so my joining of the British Veterinary Camelid Society and a very steep learning curve soon followed. Although some principles of husbandry, medicine and surgery are universal, knowledge of the idiosyncrasies of any species is crucial to the successful management of it. Most camelid lore resides in South America, and is in Spanish. Only in the relatively recent past have such eminent authors and academics such as Murray Fowler, Eric Hoffman and Walter Bravo written definitive veterinary texts on camelids in English, and these are largely based on the North American experience, as are the husbandry texts that exist.

The veterinary profession is still learning about camelids (as, indeed, it is still learning about all of the species under its care), but it became obvious to me that a basic handbook on husbandry was needed. Many of the problems commonly encountered in the keeping of llamas and alpacas could be avoided with better information, and rocket-science levels of technical sophistication are not required to circumvent most difficulties. These principles hold true for the keeping of any domestic species, but llamas and alpacas are quite frequently kept by those who have not farmed or even kept grazing animals before. The errors of experienced stock-keepers tend to be different from those committed by novices, but they nevertheless occur because of the very natural tendency to extrapolate the care of one species from that of another. Certain differences in the specialization and biology of llamas and alpacas make some such extrapolations unwise at best, and disastrous at worst. The purpose of this text is to help the uninitiated to avoid some of the more common pitfalls. There are many who will find much of the information in this book basic in the extreme, but, since my objective is to be of most help to those who need assistance most, I make no apology for the elementary level of some of it.

CHAPTER 1

Introducing Llamas and Alpacas

This chapter will briefly describe the origins of the domesticated South American camelids (i.e. llamas and alpacas) and the purposes of their domestication, and indicate some important differences between them and other domesticated animals in the UK.

Llamas and alpacas belong to a group of animals known as the South American camelids, which are descended from an ancient camel-like ancestor that migrated to the Americas millions of years ago. (The term camelid derives from their scientific family name, Camilidae.) Other camelids include the dromedary and bactrian camels. The American camelids subsequently died out in the northern part of the continent, but in the

A llama, the largest of the four South American camelids. (Photo: Chris Eke, UK Llamas)

An alpaca, the luxury fibre factory of the South American camelids. (Photo: John Gaye, Alpacas of Wessex)

A guanaco, the wild progenitor of the llama, is still found extensively in South America. (Photo: Chris Eke, UK Llamas)

A vicuna, the shy, rare, endangered progenitor of alpacas. It is found on limited ranges, mainly in the altiplano. (Photo: John Gaye, Alpacas of Wessex)

A tampuli llama. Notice the fibre on the neck and upper legs – much thicker and longer than in other llamas. (Photo: Chris Eke, UK Llamas)

A ccara llama. Notice the light fibre cover on the head, neck and legs. (Photo: Chris Eke, UK Llamas)

south they were domesticated by the Incas, and they formed the basis of the Inca economy. They were used for meat, fleece, hides, leather, tools and fuel, and as pack animals. The harsh environment of the Andes makes each of these resources truly a matter of life and death, and an animal that could thrive there was essential to human survival. When the Spaniards conquered the Inca, they seemed to make a particular campaign of

Tampuli llama. Notice the fringing on the head and ears. (Photo: Chris Eke, UK Llamas)

A selection of products that can be made from llama fibre.

attempting to exterminate llamas and alpacas. This has given rise to the idea that the Spanish may have seen such a strategy as a way of fatally weakening the much more numerous Inca.

It is generally accepted that llamas (*Lama glama*) were domesticated from the larger of the two wild camelids, the guanaco (*Lama guanicoe*), and that alpacas (*Vicugna pacos*) derived from the smaller, shyer, rarer vicuna (*Vicugna vicugna*). However, genetic studies have indicated that there has been cross-breeding in the past (possibly as a result of the disruption caused by the Spanish conquest) and all four species are capable of interbreeding and producing fertile crosses. There are no wild llamas or alpacas: they exist only as domesticated animals. There is in South America a large number of llama/alpaca-cross individuals, which are called huarizos or mistis. There are also wild populations of guanaco and vicuna. The guanaco is found extensively in South America, but the vicuna is endangered and protected. It lives in limited ranges in harsh conditions at high altitude.

LLAMAS

These are the largest of the four South American camelids, and can weigh from 110–250kg (250–550lb) and stand 102–119cm (40–47in) at the shoulder. They can be many different colours, and also a mixture of colours. There are several physical types, but their characteristics can overlap, so in a sense they are not true 'breeds'. In South America they are distinguished by whether the neck and head is woolly or fairly bare, and on the length and cover of the rest of their fibre. The woolly necked types are collectively known as tampuli, and can be further subdivided into lanuda and tapada. The lanuda is woolly on the ears and head, and further down the legs. The barer-necked ones are the short-coated ccara (or 'classic', although these are actually numerically rarer in South America) and curaca, with a medium coat. The barer-necked llamas tend to moult to a close-cropped level

of fleece. The reason for these different forms is that there is a number of different jobs for the animal to do. Pack animals will cope better with exertion if their coats are not too heavy and thick, but because the Incas made everything from ropes and bags to upholstery and clothing from fibre, some heavily fibred animals with a range of fibre types were also needed. In addition, there is considerable variation of climate, and different fleece types allow the animals to cope best with their local weather conditions.

ALPACAS

These are much smaller than llamas, weighing in at between 55 and 90kg (121 and 200lb) and reaching only 76–96cm (30–38in) at the shoulder. Twenty-two different shades of solid colour are recognized, allowing a wide range of fabric colours to be produced from the undyed fleece. There are two basic breeds, classified by fleece character: the huacaya, which has a sheep-like woolliness, and the suri, whose fleece hangs in long spiral locks. This is a true-breeding genetic difference, with the suri gene being dominant: a first cross should look like a suri, but, if crossed again with a huacaya, the result will be a 50:50 mixture of suri-looking offspring and huacaya offspring

Alpacas are the major fibre-producer. Note that it's 'not done' to call it wool. This is not merely snobbery, since the microscopic structure of the fibre is indeed different, with the individual scales from which it is composed meeting in smooth joints, like paving slabs; with wool, these scales overlap, like roof tiles. This difference translates into a different feel to the fibre and fabrics made from it, as well as different processing characteristics. Alpacas really have no function as a pack animal. They are usually shorn every year, and as the coat gets longer they find that exertion makes them overheat. They have been selected for a long, even, dense coat, which covers the neck and legs. Typically the fibre is fine, but it often coarsens with age, so a range of fibre

A suri alpaca exhibiting the classical cord-like locks. (Photo: John Gaye,, Alpacas of Wessex)

This guanaco is running for sheer pleasure. Moments later he cleared the fence behind him, illustrating one of the difficulties inherent in keeping guanacos. (Photo: Chris Eke, UK Llamas)

A huacaya alpaca showing typical woolly looking fleece. (Photo: John Gaye, Alpacas of Wessex)

diameters of 16–40 microns is found. Suri fibre is similarly fine but typically more lustrous and silky than that of the huacaya.

GUANACOS

Guanacos weigh 100–120kg (220–265lb) and grow to 76–96cm (30–38in) in height. They are all a similar colour, having a greyish head, a sandy brown topside, and a pale cream underside. Guanacos exist as wild animals in many parts of South America, but captive-born animals can be domesticated reasonably successfully. They have been used as pack animals and for their fibre, but they tend to be more wilful and will jump out of enclosures much more readily. Guanaco fibre can be very fine, at 18–24 microns, but older animals also have coarse guard hair, especially on the neck, legs and belly.

VICUNAS

These are the smallest of the four South American camelids, at only 45–55kg (100–120lb), but they are a similar height to alpacas, at 86–96cm (34–38in). They are an endangered species, and live on marginal harsh ground in the high Andes. They are protected, and are very shy, nervous animals. They have not been successfully domesticated, and in the past the only way of harvesting the fabulous fibre (often 10–14 microns in diameter) was to kill the animal. In Inca times it was a capital offence for anyone not of royal blood to wear vicuna. There are now attempts being made in Peru to gather and shear vicuna, so that the very poor people who share their environment can gain some economic advantage from them; this is also intended, presumably, to discourage poaching. The gathering

Machu Picchu, the lost city of the Incas, to whom we owe the domestication of the guanaco and vicuna, giving us llamas and alpacas. (Photo: John Gaye, Alpacas of Wessex)

operation, the Chaku, takes place every two years, and requires hundreds of people to spread across the hillside and coax the animals to run into a funnel-shaped yard, where they can be concentrated and caught for shearing. The loss of their fleece in the harsh environment places them at a certain risk, and they only yield about 500gm (1lb) fibre each. However, the value of the garments that can be made from it is so great that it is nevertheless an economically viable proposition. The local people have developed a much more positive attitude to the welfare and survival of 'their' vicuna, although there are also signs of their wishing to establish possessive rights over the animals that share their range.

THE COMMON FACTOR

The common factor in the natural history of all of these animals is the dry and harsh nature of their environment. Although cloven footed, camelids do not have hooves; instead the foot is made up of two soft digital pads (*see* photograph, Chapter 5), which spread as they take the animal's weight, making the footfall very soft on the ground. This has the great advantage that they do not poach pasture. As digesters of large amounts of poor-quality forage, they do chew the cud, but the digestive system is different from the true ruminants more traditionally kept in the UK (i.e. sheep, goats, and cattle).

CHAPTER 2

Why Llamas or Alpacas?

Why have you chosen – or why should you choose – to keep either of these animals?

The odds are that if you are contemplating keeping any of the South American camelids, you have been enchanted. The most level-headed and commercially minded of people can be bewitched by the grace, beauty, gentleness, intelligence and enormous eyes of these animals, and once this has happened they must find an excuse to keep them. This chapter is to help you with that exercise.

What do you want to do with your animals? In order to decide between llamas and alpacas you need to answer this question.

Trekking with llamas is a relaxing and enjoyable way of exploring the countryside. (Photo: Chris Eke, UK Llamas)

Do They Spit?

The behaviour of these animals is dealt with more fully in a later chapter, but this is one of the first questions asked by the uninitiated. The answer is no, and yes. A well-brought-up llama or alpaca would never deliberately spit at a person, any more than a well-brought-up dog or a horse would bite. Spitting is something that camelids properly reserve for squabbles amongst themselves. However, it is possible accidentally to get caught in the crossfire during a dispute amongst them. The other circumstances in which people are on the receiving end is where the animal concerned has not been properly trained to respect humans, and then, just as a rogue dog or horse might bite, a llama or alpaca might spit. (The spit is smelly, but on the whole less damaging than being bitten by one of these other species.)

WALKING AND TREKKING COMPANIONS

If your primary interest is in walking, then pack llamas are your best bet. They are specialized for the job of trekking fairly rough terrain carrying up to 45kg (100lb), all day if necessary. The Incas depended entirely on llamas for transporting freight in the Andes, and also used to make all their equipment from llama fibre and other products. (Alpacas like to be taken for walks, but because of their smaller size and yearly yield of fibre they are not suitable for serious haulage.)

Pack llamas are a delight to have as company on a walk, and they can carry enough for a truly decadent picnic far from the hustle and bustle of picturesque spots with motor car access. If you do visit crowded spots, you are guaranteed film-star levels of attention

The elderly, infirm – or merely decadent – can picnic in style and comfort, courtesy of their llama porters. (Photo: Chris Eke, UK Llamas)

Excursions through quiet villages amuse llamas and locals alike. The discreet toilet habits of llamas and alpacas mean that your animals will not disgrace you before their public. (Photo: Chris Eke, UK Llamas)

from any of the public that you might meet. The exercise is good for a healthy llama, and the opportunity to browse vegetation along the way is nutritionally useful, too, but the handlers must make sure that any toxic plants are avoided.

One of the most practically useful attributes of these animals is their toilet habits. They like to make and use middens. This means that once an area for urination and defecation has been established, they will return to it time and again, building up a low heap of manure. On the trail, this means that they are unlikely to foul paths or car parks. In fact, llama trekkers routinely carry a little pot of manure pellets, which they can place in a convenient spot. This stimulates the animals to go there, and inappropriate fouling is completely avoided. (Without this hint, llamas usually refuse to urinate or defecate.) So not only do your walking companions carry the spare clothes, kit and food, they are house-trained into the bargain.

Commercial llama trekking enterprises are gradually springing up in the more picturesque parts of the UK. With these, clients hire the use of the llamas and a human guide for walks ranging from a couple of hours to a full day. In some cases it may be suitable or desirable to combine this attraction with camping or bed and breakfast businesses. Llamas are easier to care for and fence than horses, do less damage to pasture and trails, and there is no requirement for the client to be able to ride.

FLOCK GUARDIANS

Gelded male llamas and some alpacas can prove effective guardians of flocks of sheep, protecting them from foxes. The animals need to be selected for aptitude and attitude, and not all individuals are suitable, but those that are can be very impressive. It should be remembered that one or more determined dogs will usually get the better of the bravest llama or alpaca, and kill it, so they are not suitable for protecting against dog attacks. However, a lone dog will usually be deterred by the fearless charge of an angry llama, and all foxes are repelled.

LAWN MOWERS

Many people choose to keep either llamas or alpacas, or both, simply to keep the grass down on a smallish plot of land. (Refer to Chapter 3 for the land requirements for South American camelids.) The animals are pleasant to look at, fairly long-lived (somewhere between ten and twenty years) much more intelligent than sheep, and don't require to be slaughtered on a regular basis (unlike sheep and cattle, which naturally 'go off fat', i.e. fatten as they mature, as they have been selected to do). Again, the feet of llamas and alpacas are easy on the land, and will leave a field unpoached and level compared to the wreckage that hoofed animals can leave behind them in wet weather.

Either llamas or alpacas will serve this function. Llamas need higher fencing and are

A Note About Guanacos and Vicunas

Guanacos are the wild, 'unimproved' ancestor of llamas. They have a very fine under-fleece and a wispy overcoat of guard hair. The under-fleece can command huge prices in the luxury fibre market if the contacts for its sale are in place and, as a result, guanacos have been farmed successfully. However, although when properly handled these animals are no more hazardous than cattle or horses, they are more wilful than most domestic livestock. One of their major drawbacks is that they are excellent and eager jumpers, and although generally shorter than llamas (76–96cm/43–45in as opposed to 102–119cm/30–38in) they will easily clear fences that llamas would not attempt.

Vicuna, the smaller alpaca ancestor are very shy, nervous animals, unsuitable for sustained contact with humans. They are listed as an endangered species by CITES (Convention on International Trade in Endangered Species), and therefore not kept domestically in the UK.

Llamas or alpacas are a beautiful and fascinating alternative to other grazers. They keep the grass down and, unlike sheep and cattle, they are not slaughtered once mature. Note the guanaco in the background. (Photo: Chris Eke, UK Llamas)

A moment of triumph when the owner's ability to judge a good animal is vindicated in the show ring. (Photo: John Gaye, Alpacas of Wessex)

slightly more difficult to handle: they know that they are big and strong, and if not properly trained and handled can present difficulties. Alpacas are no less trainable, but much more diffident and obliging, understanding that most people are stronger than they are. Frequently, uninitiated people find alpacas more appealing and less intimidating. Bear in mind that although keeping camelids will reduce the time you spend using a mower, and potentially make your grass greener, pasture management will still be required.

PETS

The attractiveness of llamas and alpacas often creates the desire in people to 'have one as a pet'. While this is entirely understandable, it is, sadly, impossible in the way that most people imagine. These animals are very highly social, and will almost literally 'die of a broken heart' if kept without the company of their kind. In fact, the ailments that kill them are usually digestive, since the stress of living alone is more likely to be expressed physically as ulceration of the stomach. Even when kept in suitable numbers, they do not make good pets in

the conventional sense. Despite their appealing looks, they do not like to be touched. They can be trained to tolerate it, but still do not look for physical contact. They have no tendency to indulge in the mutual grooming often seen in horses and cattle, so being rubbed, stroked or tickled is no treat for them. Children often want to be able to cuddle them, especially alpacas in fleece, who are so adorably woolly to look at. As animals who take their prey status very seriously, being grabbed (which is what an unwanted cuddle is for the victim) is alarming at best, and terrifying at worst.

The other problem with trying to pet camelids is manners: if you succeed in teaching an individual to accept human touch, frequently its respect for humans is lost in the process. This leads to great difficulties in handling, as the animal now feels its status to be the equal of yours and therefore has no need to cooperate with you.

None of the foregoing is to say that alpacas and llamas are not affectionate, intelligent and capable of attachment to individual people. They just do not express these things with touch. Equally, many people choose to keep alpacas or llamas simply for the pleasure of

Alpaca crias are completely irresistible, like fluffy fawns. (Photo: Peter Watson, South West Alpacas)

having them around. They develop great devotion to them and get much delight from them, but actual petting is not normally involved.

THERAPY

Both llamas and alpacas have been used to assist in therapy for a variety of mental and emotional disorders in both children and adults. Autistic children in particular have been observed to dramatically improve their ability and inclination to communicate when working with trained camelids.

FIBRE PRODUCTION

Both llamas and alpacas produce fibre, but it is alpacas that have been selected over thousands of years to produce a dense, even fleece, which should be shorn annually. Llamas have one of four types of coat (*see* Chapter 1), and the heavier-fleeced animals should be shorn for comfort when required. It is possible to make a variety of ropes, bags, hats, panniers and items of clothing from llama fibre, but generally it is too coarse and prickly for use close to the skin. The products that can be made from it require craftsmanship, and it can be rewarding to learn these ancient skills to fashion items from the fleece of your own animals.

Luxury Fibre

This is the alpaca's *raison d'être*. Cloth made from baby alpaca has almost magical qualities of softness, lightness, warmth, silky drape and lustre, which can be matched only by cashmere. Aficionados would say that it cannot be matched by anything other than vicuna. At the time of writing, the alpaca fibre industry in the UK is still somewhat embryonic. This is because there are only around 10,000 animals in the UK, and to devote an industrial mill to the different requirements of alpaca processing demands greater quantities of fleece than that number of animals can produce.

Despite the fact that a home industry in alpaca fibre is still in very early stages, the monetary value of alpacas depends very heavily on their fleeces. Those animals that possess fine dense, even, bright, stylish fibre can command very high prices indeed. People already in the alpaca industry hope that the continued selection for improved fleeces will aid in the establishment of a fully fledged commercial luxury-fibre industry.

SHOWING

Many potential owners are attracted by the idea of showing their animals. Llamas and alpacas attract a great deal of public interest

Llama show with alpaca onlookers. (Photo: Chris Eke, UK Llamas)

wherever they appear, and many shows are eager to have camelid classes because of their popularity with the public. Training and showing animals is great fun and very gratifying. It allows those owners who wish to make more of a hobby of their animals to have definite objectives towards which to work. For commercial keepers, shows are an important way to market their animals, as well as allowing them to be measured against others as a way of validating their quality.

Tourist Attraction
The very appeal that llamas and alpacas have for the public leads to their use as 'eye candy', i.e. window dressing, at country-style tourist attractions. They can fulfil this function admirably, but it is important that their welfare is a prime consideration: they do not naturally like to be petted and they do need space and grass.

Breeding and Selling
At present the population of camelid keepers in the UK is still rising and, while this continues, enterprises based on the selling of young stock to new owners can thrive. To those who have already bred livestock, this can be an attractive new venture, but basic technical knowledge about animal breeding in general and llamas and alpacas in particular will be required. If you are a novice, you need a trusted expert on call near by. Luckily there is a well-developed local breed society network, so knowledgeable advice need never be far away.

CHAPTER 3

Land and Housing

This chapter should be read in conjunction with Chapter 6 because the environment in which we keep our animals affects their behaviour, which in turn determines some of their requirements.

LAND AREA

Since camelids evolved in environments that required them to roam over vast areas of land in search of sufficient food, they are adapted for this and therefore need a certain amount of running space. The bare minimum required is 0.2ha (½ acre), and this assumes that the animals are regularly walked out for exercise. Anything less than this is too small to meet their long-term welfare needs. Confined spaces and overstocking appear to be stressful to these animals, and long-term stress has been associated with digestive ulcers (*see* Chapters 4 and 13).

As a general guide, a piece of land that can support a cow and calf – the so-called cow-calf unit (about an acre) – will provide enough forage for four to five alpacas or two to three llamas. However, as stated before, it is necessary to bear in mind that the total available space is important, since it affects the behaviour of

Mechanical pasture cleaner. Clearing middens of manure benefits both the pasture (which is not scalded by too much nitrogen), and the animals (which are protected from intestinal parasites if clearing is done on a daily basis).

Midden in use. Note posture of elimination.

the animals. They must have sufficient area to accommodate middens and, since they are highly social animals, they must never be kept alone (groups of four or more are preferable). Even though they need to be kept in groups, there must be enough space for the weaker individuals to get away from the more dominant ones, or problems with chronic bullying will develop. In practice, this means that plots of more than 0.2ha (½ acre) can usually accommodate a group of suitable individuals; at the lower end of this limit, it will be necessary to select them individually for compatibility.

Ground Conditions

Alpacas and llamas are sure-footed and can cope with fairly rough ground. However, stony ground can cause the toenails to break off if they have been softened by wet weather. Swampy ground is not suitable because it causes the feet to become very softened, and the toenails will rapidly overgrow. Wet ground is also much more likely to support the freshwater snail, which carries liver fluke (a parasite to which llamas and alpacas are very susceptible). Wet areas in an otherwise dry paddock

will not be a problem, if due regard is paid to the potential for liver fluke (*see* Chapter 13).

Pasture debris such as rubbish and pieces of metal should not be allowed to remain on the ground; they will cause injury.

Middens

Llamas and alpacas create and use specific dung areas in their fields, often called middens. This makes picking up the manure a much easier job than it is with horses and other animals, and can have benefits in reducing parasite burdens on the pasture. The manure makes excellent garden fertilizer. The midden area is very nitrogen-rich, and its centre will usually kill vegetation if left undisturbed. The edges will produce superlush growth which is normally rejected by the animals for feeding unless they are very short of grazing. A rather patchy-looking pasture can result from the presence of middens, but they probably have a certain anti-parasitic function: worm larvae are concentrated in the dung areas and, because these are avoided by grazing llamas and alpacas, the opportunity to become further infested with worms is reduced. If you collect the manure

Plain high-tensile wire with low-level netting is adequate fencing, but the upper wires will gradually become slackened if they are regularly challenged by leaning males.

Post-and-rail fencing – made cria-proof with sheep netting low down – keeps this amorous male separate from the females.

from the middens, and compost it, the larvae should die in a few months, making the resultant compost safe to re-spread on the fields. If you simply harrow the middens to spread them out, you will spread worm larvae with them. If the winter is cold enough to freeze the ground hard, almost all of the worm larvae will be killed, and the pasture can be regarded as 'clean', as long as it has been unstocked. Grazing animals will reinfest it if they are carrying overwintering worms inside them.

Predators

It is much easier to keep llamas and alpacas in than it is to keep dogs and badgers out, yet in their respective ways both of these predators can represent lethal threats to your animals. You do not want to be in the position of having contained your animals so effectively that marauding dogs can catch and savage them easily. This is more of a problem in North America where free-ranging dogs are more common, but it is a consideration in certain parts of the UK. In the case of badgers, there is evidence from Ireland that they can infect llamas and alpacas with TB (as they have long been suspected of doing in cattle). Contact with badgers should therefore be prevented. It is no easy matter to achieve this, since badgers are powerful and determined, and will tunnel or barge their way through many types of barrier. The most effective means of excluding them appears to be a triple strand of electric fencing placed at low level, and while this may seem an expensive investment it is cheap in comparison to the cost of having tuberculosis infect your animals. DEFRA (the Department of Environment, Farming and Rural Affairs) should be able to advise on badger proofing. Badgers are currently protected, which means that active destruction of them or their setts is illegal.

Picturesque and indigenous, but a potential TB hazard. (Photo: Paula Hanley)

Midden discipline is not absolute, and some individuals, especially youngsters, will defecate almost anywhere.

Poaching

The soft digital pad of camelids (*see* page 53) causes far less damage to soft ground and vegetation than occurs with hoofed livestock, which cause poaching (muddy, water-filled holes in wet ground). Poaching results in less available grazing because the grass becomes mashed into the mud. My grandfather used to say that in wet weather cows have five mouths because of the extra pressure on the vegetation caused by poaching.

FENCING

Camelids are easy to fence. It is not in their nature to barge or wriggle through fencing like sheep or pigs, push it over like cattle, or jump it. Consequently, almost any fencing system that will contain other domestic livestock will contain llamas and alpacas. The exceptions to this general rule are crias (babies) separated from their mothers, and animals that are terrified (and this includes separation from their group) or in love (i.e. males in pursuit of receptive females). The other exception is guanacos or their crosses, who are excellent and enthusiastic jumpers.

Barbed wire can cut animals, if they try to escape, and snag fleece. Barbed wire is not really necessary for llamas and alpacas because they don't make a habit of leaning on fencing (as cattle do) and, if they panic enough to try to get out, the barbs will not deter them. (The drawbacks of barbed wire apply to other species no less than to camelids.)

Plain high-tensile wire can work well, although, because it is hard to see, animals may run into it until they know it is there. Plain wires will not contain crias. Wire sheep fencing is good at preventing cria escape, but can trap limbs if a youngster tries to wriggle through, which if separated from its mother it will certainly do.

Post-and-rail fencing is attractive and effective if combined with wire sheep-fencing at low level, but always beware of crowding animals up to any fence with potentially limb-trapping gaps.

Hedges will suffice as llama and alpaca fencing if properly maintained, but they should not contain any poisonous plants because they will be browsed. If gaps are allowed to appear, the animals will simply walk through them. Generally a secondary barrier of wire fencing is required for adequate security.

Electric fencing can be a convenient and cheap means of subdividing pasture, but it should be used only in the expectation that sooner or later an animal will run through it and may become entangled. Electric tape is probably better than electric wire because it is easier for the animal to see and less likely to cut into the flesh in entanglement incidents. Because it is very likely that electric fencing systems will fail for some reason at some point, single-strand fences are unsuitable for boundary fencing, or for situations where escape would be disastrous.

WATER

Fresh water should be available at all times, although healthy animals who are not feeding crias will often choose not to drink very much. Normal stock troughs are adequate, and these should be kept clean and serviced as for any livestock. More elaborate drinkers will require a training period for the animals to learn how to use them, and some take to this more readily than others. Raised troughs prevent badgers from using the water.

Llamas and alpacas like streams, and will readily paddle and wallow in hot weather, but persistent wallowing will wreck fleece. With natural water sources, it should be remembered that animals, especially young ones, can fall off ledges, or get stuck in mud or other hazards. Trekking llamas will frequently defecate in running water, so the possibility of their fouling a stream should be considered if that is their only water source, as should the use if it by wildlife, especially badgers. Llamas and alpacas will not normally drink dirty or polluted water, but young animals will do almost any stupid thing, including that one.

VEGETATION

Camelids are very forage efficient. That is to say, they do not need a lush, productive sward to be happy and healthy; they can digest fairly poor, fibrous forage. This means that they can be kept on fairly poor, marginal pasture, and do not require the specialized ryegrass and clover leys typical of the intensively kept food-producing animals.

The split upper lip of llamas and alpacas is mobile and very sensitive, and allows highly selective food choice. They browse eagerly, and hedges will show a distinct cropped line marking the height that they can reach. They will browse a variety of hedgerow plants, including the leaves of brambles and dog rose (and unfortunately they frequently get the thorny sticks entangled in their fleeces). They tend to reject very long grass, and they do not usually eat thistles, nettles, docks or buttercups (which are irritant and cause mouth and lip sores), so some pasture management is required and these weeds should be controlled or else they will gradually take over

Alpacas on the altiplano in Peru. Contrast this harsh environment with that shown in the photograph below. (Photo: John Gaye, Alpacas of Wessex)

Even in early winter, pasture in the UK is much more lush than that generally found on the altiplano. (Photo: John Gaye, Alpacas of Wessex)

Healthy alpacas and llamas can cope with normal British weather conditions without difficulty. (Photo: Peter Watson, South West Alpacas)

Poisonous Plants

Llamas and alpacas should not be allowed to come into contact with plants that are known to be poisonous to other livestock, such as rhododendron and yew. Bracken is thought to be poisonous to them, but they seem in any case not to eat it. The problem with such plants is that they can become palatable at certain times of the year, and if animals have access to them they may suddenly decide to start eating them, with disastrous results. Ragwort, which is extremely poisonous, is just such a plant: it is unpalatable while it is growing, but if it is incorporated into hay and dried it will be eaten. When acorns first drop camelids will eat them greedily. Again, we would expect them to be poisonous, and should discourage the consumption of large amounts, even though reported poisoning incidents seem to be rare.

the pasture. Certain individuals will indulge in experimental food choices; in other words, they will try anything. Because they are not evolved for our vegetation, they are likely to graze toxic plants, so the only safe poisonous plant is one that is kept away from them.

Llamas and alpacas are happy with a diet composed mainly of grasses. They prefer pastures that contain a mix of species. They are not especially keen on Italian ryegrass, one of the major components of modern British grass leys. Mature permanent pasture is probably most ideal because it has had time for deeper-rooted species to develop, and these will probably have a higher mineral content (*see* Chapter 4). When the pasture is growing quickly, it will often exceed the animals' appetite and requirements, and they will become more selective, allowing some areas to grow long and go to seed. The food value of this grass drops greatly during the maturation process, and the long areas should be 'topped', i.e. have the tops mown off. This keeps the sward more palatable and nutritious. During the rapid grass growth of the summer, it may be best to fence off some of the pasture and take a hay crop from it (if you have sufficient space for the animals to get enough grass on a smaller area). During the winter, the grass will virtually stop growing, and lose much of its feed value, so the hay will be required as supplemental feeding.

HOUSING AND YARDS

Under normal conditions, healthy llamas and alpacas have no requirement for housing in the UK. Their coats are weatherproof and they can live successfully outside all year round. This does assume that they will have shelter from the sun and wind, when necessary, from hedges, fences or trees. However, there are some instances in which you will find purpose-built shelters of various sorts useful:

• Husbandry procedures.
There are various aspects of husbandry that require the animals to be restrained and handled – for example, for toenail trimming, injections, worming and shearing. Shearing can be done only in dry conditions, and you won't do the other things in the rain many times before you wish you had a shed. Fleece will heat and rot if stored damp. (If the fleece does get damp, it must be dried before being bagged.) Even in the summer the dew will wet the surface of the fleece, and keeping the animals to be shorn early in the day under cover overnight will ensure that their coats are dry in the morning. Otherwise, even in good weather, you can waste half of the day while they dry off; this will not please your shearer, to whom time is money – and probably your money.

• Sick animals or weak crias.
Sooner or later an animal will become unwell, or a cria will be born during inclement weather, and protection from the elements may become a matter of life and death for it.

• Unrelenting bad weather or very severe weather.
In regions where it can rain very persistently, the keepers of alpacas and llamas usually find that it is useful to be able to put

An example of well-designed accommodation and handling facilities. Note the abundance of configurations possible (see also layout diagram on page 31) and the incorporation of sheds, allowing handling in reasonable comfort even if it is raining.

Overview of outer area of UK Llamas' yards. (Photo: Chris Eke, UK Llamas)

Galvanized movable catch pen. This pen runs on castors, and is therefore suitable for concreted yards. It greatly increases the ease with which animals can be caught and trained, because it is too tall for a llama to attempt to jump it, and small enough to make the animal easy to catch. (Photo: Chris Eke, UK Llamas)

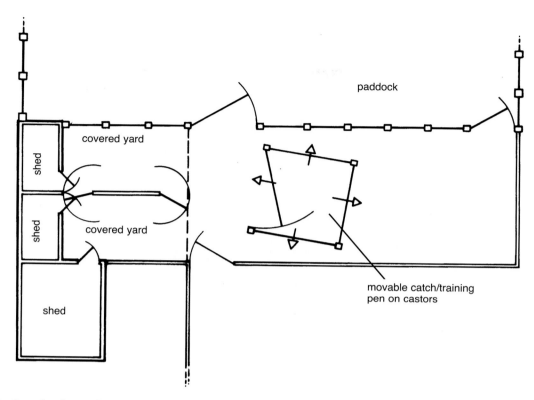

Layout of yards pictured on page 29 and opposite. Note movable tall catch pen on castors.
This feature makes the training of llamas much easier.

the animals under cover so that their fleeces do not remain wet for weeks on end. The parts of South America where they evolved are, after all, arid, and it would be reasonable to expect their coats literally to rot under long-term wet conditions, as well as their feet becoming very soft and prone to damage. Camelid fleece has its own grease, called suint, but there is much less of it than the typical amount of lanolin found in sheep fleece. As a result, the fleeces are less resistant to water. Suri animals, whose fleeces hang down in long ringlet-like locks, have a permanent parting down the middle of their backs, and this makes them less tolerant of wet, cold and strong sun.

Sheds

The design of the shed must be suited to its particular uses, and these are too various for hard and fast rules. However, if you are building a new structure, you have the opportunity to make it as convenient and efficient as possible. Ask yourself the following questions:

1. How many animals must it accommodate at once?
   For the short periods required for handling and husbandry procedures, each animal will need approximately 3sq. m (3½sq. yd) for alpacas and 6sq. m (7sq. yd) for llamas, plus the area you will need to work in.

2. For how long?
   If they are to be kept inside for longer periods, calculations become more difficult, since the make-up of the groups and individual natures of the animals concerned begin to have an effect. If they are overcrowded, they will bully each other, and

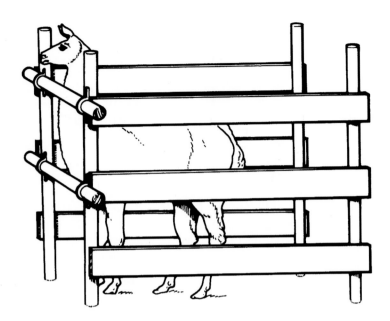

A simple restraint chute. It needs to be sturdy and tall enough to discourage an animal from jumping out. Brackets along a mid-height rail will allow a breech pole to be placed across the entrance, preventing the animal from running backwards. Forward restraint can be achieved by tying the animal to both stanchions (cross-tying), or to poles across the front. Sides, if not solid, should not have gaps that make trapping a limb likely.

individuals will become stressed; the weaker ones will probably fail to get enough food or water.

3. How often?
   Dirt floors are adequate for a few uses a year, but they are very difficult to keep clean if they are in regular use.

4. Do I need to get equipment or machines in and out as well?
   This will affect how large your doors or gates need to be, the material used for the floor, and where the building is sited.

5. Where will the air come from?
   If much time is to be spent inside, good ventilation from well placed (usually high) vents will be important, both for health and for cooling. If the building is to be used as a 'sick bay' then it must be airy, sheltered and light enough to promote convalescence.

6. Is lighting necessary?
   If natural light sources are lacking or poor, an electricity supply is essential. Alpacas and llamas prefer well-lit areas, presum-

ably because they are prey animals and feel the need to see potential predators. It has also been observed that they continue to feed during the night in lit buildings. This may be important in ensuring adequate feeding during winter, when the daylight hours are quite short.

7. How many subdivisions?
   If you are intending to use your shed for husbandry procedures, you will need a holding pen, a working area, and possibly another pen for those individuals who have had the treatment. Gates that swing in both directions and/or form the side of a pen are useful refinements, but the sophistication of your equipment becomes more important if you have more than just a few animals to handle. Sick animals will need either to be able to see their companions in the adjacent pasture or to have a companion animal visible in the next pen.

8. Is a water supply necessary?
   If you need to hospitalize an animal, or clean the building, plentiful running water is a great help.

9. How much head room?

Frightened animals can rear and plunge, so your ceiling/beam height should be above about 2.5m (8ft) for alpacas and 4m (13ft) for llamas.

Handling Yards

The first function of handling yards is to enable you to catch and restrain your animals. Camelids are prey animals and share a potent 'step away' reflex (discussed in Chapter 6). This effectively means that almost all individuals will avoid being caught if they have the space to run. Corralling them into a small yard (catch pen) where they can see that they can't get away is often all that is required to help them make the decision to stand and allow you to hold them. At the least, it means that you are able to catch them, even if they attempt to step away.

The functions of yards overlap with those of the building. For low numbers of animals, where you can largely decide when you will do your procedures depending on the weather, a simple covered sheltered area plus a more elaborate yard system will suffice.

How elaborate the design of handling yards needs to be depends on what you will require of them. They should be sited such that it is easy to tempt (with food) or drive your animals into them, and from them into the building.

A frightened, distressed or amorous llama or alpaca may well try to jump out of a yard. The sides should be at least 1.5m (5ft) high to keep alpacas in, and 2m (6½ft) for llamas. Some individuals may still attempt to jump out, but few will be capable of it. Lower barriers will often work as long as the animals do not particularly want to escape, but if they get stuck on the top of fencing they can injure themselves badly, so it is a situation best avoided. Remember that guanacos and their crosses are much more able and enthusiastic jumpers, so even if they are the same size as alpacas, fence them as though they are llamas!

Ideally, your yards should have a larger holding area into which it is not difficult to persuade your animals, and an adjoining smaller catch pen – 2.5 × 3m (8 × 10ft), for example – where you can lay hold of them easily. Supervised matings can take place in either sized yard.

Footing

This should be non-slippery (including when wet) and cleanable if there will be frequent use. Concrete is the most hygienic, but is quite hard on the legs of the animals if the yards are used for matings. (*See* Chapter 10.)

Restraint Chutes

There are many designs of these in use, mainly in North America. They can be very helpful when performing husbandry procedures on untrained and uncooperative animals, but there are currently no patented mass-produced ones available, so you will have to have your own constructed if you decide that you want one.

A simple race with high sides (constructed with boarding attached to the rails), and secure closure at each end has worked well for me.

CHAPTER 4

Feeding and Nutrition

What do llamas and alpacas eat? Grass, is the short answer, but keep reading, because it's not the whole answer, especially not in the UK. A simple grass diet, which will keep them alive in the short term, will not necessarily keep them healthy in the long term.

Alpacas and llamas are bulk feeders, evolved to survive on poor forage in relatively harsh conditions. This means that they are specialized to eat and digest lots of minimally nutritious forage. In other words, they expect to have to eat a lot of their food to stay fat. They therefore have a skeleton that is capable of ranging over long distances (in order to search for food) and they are provided with teeth that are gradually extruded until the age of about seven (in the expectation that all the chewing they will have to do will wear them down). They also have a very long gut tube with a slow passage time to allow efficient extraction of nutrients. They are resistant to the high mineral levels found in the deep-rooted plants of their natural range, and browse (i.e. eat non-grass plants) readily. Their body condition is naturally lean and fluctuates throughout the year depending on food supply and physiological drain, that is to say whether they are burning energy keeping warm, feeding a cria, growing a pregnancy, defending and chasing females or finding food.

Most of us do not mimic these conditions for our animals. We tend to keep them in small fields on relatively lush pasture. The soft, nutritious plants in these pastures provide lots of energy and protein, but less fibre and less bulk than the animals are adapted for, and, being shallow rooted, also give lower levels of minerals than they need, too. On top of that most of us feed some sort of concentrate in the form of pellets or muesli-type mix. The nutritional features of these foods are that they are low bulk, high calorie, high starch and protein, and, usually, high mineral content.

The whole digestive system is specialized to deal with a long fibrous diet, and depends upon it for health. (Llamas and alpacas are not true ruminants, like sheep, goats and cattle. Even though they chew the cud, the arrangement of their stomachs is different.) So, grass, hay, haylage – what is termed 'long forage' because the plant stems are long – should comprise 85–90 per cent of the diet.

DIGESTION

The plant energy stored in the fibre of the diet is released via a process of digestion by microscopic organisms (a mixture of fungi, protozoa and bacteria, collectively known as the gut microflora, or gut flora), which inhabit the fermentation chambers of the stomach. These chambers are known as C1, C2 and C3. C3 is the largest (accounting for about 10–15 per cent of the animal's weight). Only part of C3 resembles our stomach. The chemicals produced by the micro-organisms are then absorbed through the stomach wall to nourish the animal. The activity of this microflora is responsible for the greatest part of the animal's nutrition, producing energy-rich volatile fatty acids, protein, vitamins, especially of the B group, as well as gas. When we feed our animals, we are really feeding a vast microbial factory, without which the llama or alpaca could not survive.

In order for the microbial factory to thrive, it needs a suitable environment. The fermentation process requires a site away from oxygen (since it is anaerobic), and a continuous supply of raw materials (i.e., grass and water), which have been ground up (by chewing and cudding). These are then mixed by contractions, and have the fermentation products removed before the concentration of them reaches toxic levels. Feeding strategies should always take consideration of their effect on the gut flora.

Chewing the Cud/Rumination

This is a process whereby a mouthful of coarsely chewed forage is regurgitated from C1 or C2 back up to the mouth and chewed again. It improves the degree to which the plant fibre is ground up, and helps the microbes attack it for digestion. The addition of more saliva also aids digestion, and the contractions of C1 and C2, which occur during cud chewing, improve the mixing of the fermentation 'soup'. Camelids will ruminate when relaxed, for up to eight hours every day, usually during daylight. The higher the fibre content of the diet, the longer the animal will chew the cud. If your llama or alpaca is in pain, has a fever, has too much acidity or gas in the fermentation chamber, or a low level of calcium in the blood, rumination will decrease or stop.

Further digestion of protein and fat happens along the digestive tract, beginning in a part of the stomach that resembles yours and mine a bit more (part of C3). The efficiency of digestion, and the health of the vital lining of the gut, depend on the correct level of acidity inside the gut. Without a stable mat of chewed plant fibre and micro-organisms, the acidity of the gut tends to increase, and in any case becomes less easy to regulate. This

can lead to a tendency for ulcers to form on the stomach lining.

PASTURE

In the summer, pasture can meet most of the needs of llamas and alpacas, provided there is enough of it. Nevertheless it is a good idea to provide access to hay also, since when green grass is quite lush it does not really have sufficient fibre in it. Having said that, llamas and alpacas often eat very little hay when grass is plentiful.

Very lush pastures can cause the animals to have diarrhoea. This occurs because there is an excess of soluble nutrients, water and a lack of fibre, which conspire to upset the gut flora and cause more water to be retained in the faeces. It can be a good idea either to put the animals on poorer pasture during the early part of the summer, if it is available, or to limit their grazing area to reduce the amount of lush grass they can eat. (Note that summer diarrhoea can also be the result of parasitic worms – *see* Chapter 13.)

Because the high-altitude pastures in the Andes are nutritionally rather poor, problems in Britain frequently centre around abundance. Our grasses are softer, more nutritious, higher in soluble sugars and shallower-rooted. This combination means that compared to the diet for which llamas and alpacas evolved, UK grasses yield more energy for less grazing effort, and far less mineral content. The animals get less exercise because they do not need to walk so far to get enough food, and they will be satisfied with less bulk because the sward is more nutritious. It is very common to see llamas and alpacas in the UK become fat, and yet still suffer mineral deficiency disease because the mineral levels in our pasture are much lower, and they need to consume less pasture to assuage their hunger. The effect of these two factors is that they eat less forage, which has a lower mineral content anyhow, and can become deficient.

Alpacas on long, untopped weedy pasture have been observed to select cow parsley and cut nettles. Often the rougher and less 'improved' the pasture, the better, although hay should always be available. The reason for this is that 'pasture improvement' usually involves a reduction of the number of species in a sward. The species favoured by farmers of other domestic livestock are shallow rooted and ideally suited to respond to chemical fertilizers with rapid growth. This produces a high-energy, high-protein sward with a low mineral content (because of the rapid growth and shallow roots of the grasses). This type of pasture is unlikely to suit alpacas and llamas well, and you should expect deficiencies to develop.

Although rough grazing has its advantages, bear in mind that in general, alpacas and llamas won't eat docks, thistles or nettles, and if they are not controlled by topping or chemicals, these could eventually take over the whole pasture.

WATER

It is easy, in a wet climate such as the UK's, to forget the importance of water. Although adapted for arid conditions, llamas and alpacas cannot survive without adequate fresh water. The greater the dry matter intake (*see*

Dry Matter

Dietary discussions where animals are concerned tend to be on what is called 'dry matter basis'. This means that any weights of food referred to are of the food with all the water removed. This is useful, because water, although vital, is not a food, and many foods and forages can have highly variable water content, so by talking about dry matter we can compare foods from an equal starting point. On the other hand, it makes measuring 'as fed' food tricky, unless you know what the water content is. For example, typically, grass will have a water content of 50–80 per cent depending upon the time of year, prevailing weather, type of grass, etc. Hay, on the other hand, has around 10–12 per cent water.

---

box), the more water the animal needs to maintain the healthy balance of the microbial fermentation mat in C1, as well as for the physiological functions shared by all mammals.

Llamas and alpacas need 5–8 per cent of their bodyweight in water every day. For example, a 70kg (155lb) alpaca needs 3.5–5.5 litres (1 gallon) of water a day. Green pasture already contains up to 80 per cent water, but hay has only about 10 per cent. Animals need more water when they are having to survive on drier foods.

Body processes consume water, so animals that are active, hot, growing, pregnant or lactating need extra water over their basic gallon or so. Milk is 87 per cent water, so an equal volume to that produced must be consumed by the mother animal. Plentiful fresh water should always be available, even to young crias and, if you are transporting your animals, plan to provide adequate water at rest stops or, in the case of short trips, at the journey's end.

ESSENTIAL ELEMENTS

The essential components of an animal's diet are – in addition to water – energy, protein, fibre, vitamins, and minerals.

Protein
All animals need some element of protein in their diet, since it forms the structural elements of living organisms. Therefore growth, repair, pregnancy and activity all require it. The microbes get their protein from the plant cells in the diet, which they digest in the fermentation chambers of C1 and C2 and turn into microbial protein. Microbial cells pass on down the digestive tract and are digested and absorbed in their turn.

Alpacas and llamas are selective grazers; this is a behavioural adaptation to the poor pastures on which they have evolved. Research that has been carried out has revealed that when grazing a pasture whose herbage had an average protein content of 10

Protein Requirements

Protein requirements depend on the life stage of an animal and will fluctuate over its life time. The protein requirements of various types of stock have been measured in other species, and for them are approximately:

Maintenance	8–10%
Gestation	12%
Lactation	13–15%
Growth <9 months	12–14%
Growth >9–18 months	10–12%

(Ref. Jane Vaughan, Alpaca World *Winter 2004/5)*

per cent, the contents of C1 had a protein content of 15 per cent.

The protein in the diet is usually expressed as Crude Protein, or CP. It is called 'crude' because it merely measures the amount of nitrogen and multiplies it by 6.25, assuming that all the nitrogen is making up its usual 16 per cent of protein. The amount of this that can be broken down by the microbes is called Rumen Degradable Protein (RDP) and includes both real protein and other nitrogenous compounds, such as urea, which are more highly soluble and easily utilized. Some of the protein is not broken down by the microbes; it passes on into the rest of the digestive system where it is broken down by that. This leftover protein is called Undegraded Dietary Protein (UDP) – or Bypass Protein (because it has effectively bypassed the fermentation process).

The amount of RDP that the animal can possibly utilize depends on the amount, health and activity of the microbial mat, but so-called Bypass Protein can provide additional protein for the animal not dependent on microbial processes.

The protein content of different feeds is very variable; forage feeds (grass, hay, haylage, silage) especially are so variable that you really need to have them analysed to know what level your animals are getting.

Rapidly growing, bright green pasture has more protein (typically from 15–30 per cent – in DM, remember) than more mature, late-season sward, where protein can decline to a third of its peak level. Hay also varies in protein level, with alfalfa/lucerne hay containing 10–20 per cent and grass meadow hay having only about 8 per cent. Early-cut hay is better than late-cut. Clover hay is relatively high protein (11 per cent) but it is quite fragile and tends to break up to dust easily in handling, so it can be difficult to source. Cereal grains (e.g. oats, wheat) can be from 8–13 per cent protein, but the pea family, e.g. lupins, are much higher at 25–45 per cent.

If you look back at the overall protein content required at different times of life, you can see that relying on grass or hay alone will leave certain classes of animal deficient in protein.

Minerals

The minerals story is not exactly simple, either. How much and what, depends upon what your animals are doing for you, and what your forage already provides. Llamas and alpacas appear to have a very high requirement for, or tolerance to (depending upon how you look at it), certain minerals that occur at variable levels in most of Britain, i.e. calcium, phosphorus, magnesium, zinc, copper, cobalt, selenium.

This means that in addition to their forage, these animals will require some form of supplemental feeding, largely to address their mineral requirements. What they require, and how much of it, depends upon what is in the local forage. To know exactly what your animals are likely to need, pasture analysis is necessary. Without it, you are guessing to an extent.

The other consideration is that llamas and alpacas cannot tolerate large amounts of concentrated feed. Therefore the inclusion rate of mineral supplements in the feed has to be much higher than for other livestock species, which eat more. This in turn creates problems because correctly supplemented llama

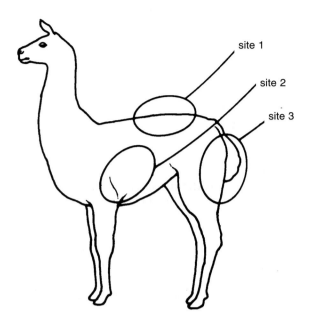

Sites for palpation or observation of body fat stores to arrive at a condition score.

and alpaca feed would be toxic for other live-stock species to consume in the quantities they usually eat. Feed-mill owners are reluctant to make up batches of camelid feeds because they have to clean down the whole production line before the next batch of feed for another species.

HOW MUCH FOOD?

One animal will vary from another in how much food of any type it requires to maintain acceptable condition. In order to judge how well your chosen diet is doing this for your animals you must learn to condition score.

Condition Scoring
Condition scoring is a hands-on (literally) method of assessing how much fat-cover an animal has. It is a vital method for measuring the success of your feeding programme, because once your animals have a reasonable degree of fleece cover it is impossible to tell how fat or thin they are just by looking. The

two major sites to get your hand on to feel are over the loins and down the ribs at the side of the chest

Various scales of numbers are used, most commonly 0–5 or 1–10, so it is important to make sure that any recorded measurements actually state, e.g. CS 4 out of 5 or CS 4 out of 10. An ideal condition score is around 3.5 to 4, out of 5 but it is normal for each animal to fluctuate over the course of the year. One that is condition score 4 out of 5 in the depths of the winter while feeding a cria is probably going to spend most of the year far too fat. Conversely, an animal that goes down to 2.5 out of 5 at its lowest, need not necessarily be cause for alarm if it recovers to 3.5 out of 5 for the most part of the year. When assessing condition scores, take into account what the animal is trying to do: e.g. feeding a cria, coping with winter, and what its grazing companions are, too. If they are all much the same and not dangerously under or over weight, there's less to worry about than if one is very different from the rest.

Weighing scales are more accurate than condition scoring, and larger enterprises will have and use them. For keepers of fewer animals, catching each individual once a month and condition scoring it will provide vital monitoring of your feeding plan. It is a good idea to get into the habit of condition scoring any animal that you catch. You cannot manage the nutrition of your alpacas or llamas adequately unless you condition score or weigh them regularly.

WHO NEEDS WHAT?

Gelded or fully grown bachelor males require far less complicated nutrition than breeding females, who are undoubtedly the biggest challenge. If you want your females to calve every year, it means that they spend most of the year pregnant and lactating. The nutrients consumed by these processes must come from somewhere. Growing youngstock come somewhere in between in terms of nutritional demand. The point is that you need to

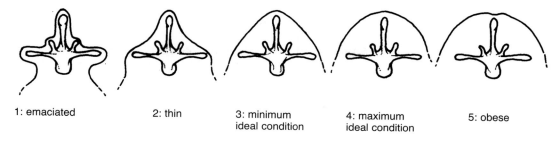

| 1: emaciated | 2: thin | 3: minimum ideal condition | 4: maximum ideal condition | 5: obese |

Schematic representation of the cross-section of the lumbar spine, showing the underlying bones – which can be felt (or not) in condition scoring.

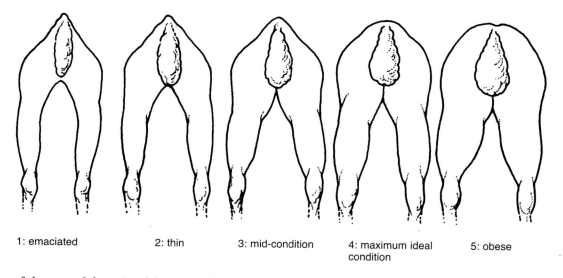

| 1: emaciated | 2: thin | 3: mid-condition | 4: maximum ideal condition | 5: obese |

View of the rear of the animal from which the degree of fat cover in between the legs can be seen. This view is helpful only in lightly fibred animals.

make an assessment of each individual's nutritional requirements.

Geldings and Adult Bachelor Males.
The accepted amount of food that a llama or alpaca can eat is 1.4–1.8 per cent bodyweight on a dry matter basis, so any calculations must take account of the water content as it is fed. Since much early-season pasture is 70–80 per cent water, they will have to consume from 10lb (for a smallish alpaca) up to 13kg (28lb) of pasture (for a full-sized llama) to meet this requirement. That is a pretty big heap of grass. Obviously they will eat less hay, typical-

ly 1–2kg (2–5lb), which is useful because generally we don't (and can't) weigh the grass they eat, but we do have to weigh (and haul) hay.

Nursing Mothers
If a female llama is feeding a 23kg (50lb) cria that is gaining 0.25kg (½lb) daily, she must have, in addition to her maintenance requirement for food, the wherewithal to produce around 2.5kg (80oz) milk per day. In the milk there will be 4gm calcium, 3gm phosphorus, and 10gm protein. Most forages will not be sufficient to meet these requirements, leaving mineral deficits of about 60 per cent in

the case of calcium and phosphorus, and 90 per cent for selenium and zinc. Obviously in the long term this drain on the animal's resources will start to affect her health, body condition and fertility.

Rich, rapidly growing pasture may well meet the nursing mother's protein and energy needs, but as the sward matures (within weeks of its peak nutritional value) she will find it more and more difficult to eat enough to keep up. It should be remembered that although alpacas and llamas need a fibrous diet, beyond a certain level of fibre the time taken to eat and digest it starts to prevent them from getting enough of it (the microbes take longer to break down more fibrous diets, and these therefore move through the digestive tract more slowly).

Supplementary feed will need to be supplied to balance the lack of calcium, phosphorus, selenium and zinc. On all but the most productive sward, extra energy and protein will also be needed.

DIETS

Concentrates

Reasons for feeding concentrated foods are:

1. To fill in any deficiencies in the diet;
2. Because it makes it easy to check and handle the animals on a daily basis (the foods are palatable so the animals will come to you to be fed).

If your animals are already in good condition, i.e. condition score 3 or more on a 0–5 scale, or 5–6 on a 0–9 scale, they don't need extra energy and protein. The only thing they need from the supplementary feed is minerals, which they may not get in sufficient quantity from forage alone. Bear in mind that bachelor males and geldings rarely need any concentrate feed.

It is very useful to establish acceptance of concentrate food because, especially in the winter, it is often the only way to get extra calories and minerals into them. Having said that, don't get carried away and feed them too much of it: fatness does not equal health in these animals. The skill in feeding therefore lies in getting sufficient minerals into them without feeding too much concentrate. They should always have access to good-quality hay to encourage them to keep up their fibre intake.

In the UK, there are many supplementary feeds available, but almost all of them are formulated for other species, and are deficient in some areas and too rich in others with respect to the requirements of llamas and alpacas. In addition, they may have added elements that are positively harmful for our animals. These include high levels of oils and fats, which they do not digest well, and too-concentrated energy sources, such as ground or whole grains. When these are digested by camelids, they can cause a too-acid environment for the vital gut flora, and damage the gut, promoting the formation of ulcers and liver disease.

I do not know of any successful keepers of llamas and alpacas who do not use a supplementary feed formulated especially for them. These feeds are relatively expensive because a feed mill must be devoted to producing that food only. When the batch is finished, the mill must be cleaned down so that there is no possibility of contaminating the feed of other animals (which may be poisoned by the high mineral content of llama and alpaca feed). However, it is important to keep in mind the possible price of penny-pinching on feed. If your animals become malnourished, at the very best they will not produce or perform so well, and at worst will be susceptible to disease. Under-performance can be quite difficult to measure in financial terms, since it can be difficult to know, for example, how many more days it took you to get a female pregnant, or how much better a cria would have looked in the ring if better nourished.

There are currently available a handful of specialist camelid feeds: Carr's and Camelibra were the first, and others have now been formulated. As far as we know, they are equally good at supplying the all-important mineral supplementation that is needed, especially by breeding females, but Carr's will also provide more calories, being molassed. If your animals are inclined to fatness, a lower energy feed, such as Camelibra, may be the better bet for them, but if they are lactating (milking) heavily and struggling to maintain condition, then a molassed feed such as Carr's may be the answer.

At the time of writing there is a number of fairly easily available feeds formulated for llamas and alpacas. Details of some of them follow, and comparison of the information supplied by the feed companies shows differences both in what they contain and in the information supplied with them. It is not possible absolutely to say that one product is better than another, and the choice you make for your animals depends upon their situation, the nutrients provided by their forage, and what they are doing for you. Generally, successful llama and alpaca supplementary feeds contain higher levels of minerals than are included in cattle and sheep feeds.

Billington Carr's Camelid Care Coarse Mix.
This feed is specifically designed for animals on forage-rich diets. That is to say, it is designed to complement a bulky diet that has insufficient nutrient density for the physical demands of lactation or growth. It has very high levels of minerals and vitamins to ensure that the whole diet, including the forage element, will be balanced. Protein level is 14 per cent. The vitamin, mineral and trace element profile is as follows:

Vitamin A	40,000iu/kg
Vitamin D3	16,000iu/kg
Vitamin E	200iu/kg
Thiamine (B1)	80iu/kg
Vitamin B12	120iu/kg
Manganese	500mg/kg
Zinc	1,000mg/kg
Copper	65mg/kg
Cobalt	8mg/kg
Iodine	25mg/kg
Selenium	2mg/kg
Calcium	2.4%

Feed Bin Security

Feed bin security is important whatever the feed mix you use, as is accurately measuring the amount that is eaten by each animal. However, some feeds in particular can, if overfed, cause acute problems of grain overload (principally acidosis, *see* Chapter 13) and chronic ones of mineral toxicity. If an individual animal gains access to the storage bin, it may well gorge dangerous amounts.

Phosphorus	1.6%
Sodium	0.5%
Salt	1.3%

This feed is one of the muesli types, which uses molasses, sugar beet pulp, flaked peas, beans and grains to make it palatable, and most animals accept it eagerly. Because of the molasses and grains, it is relatively high in energy and protein, and should be used for lactating females that require more energy and that have difficulty in eating enough grass to get it (so called 'bulk limiting' where the animal simply cannot deal with the physical quantity of food it would require at that level of nutrient density).

Accurate measuring of rations and feed bin security is especially important with this feed (*see* box this page).

Camelibra
This feed comes in the form of a very finely milled pellet, similar to those fed to poultry. It is also formulated specifically for camelids, but has much less grain and molasses so, as a supplement, it has less energy. This makes it suitable for those animals that are not having any difficulty maintaining weight – for example, bachelor and working males, growing youngstock, pregnant maiden females.

It contains Biosaf viable cells of Cerevisiae strain Sc 47, which increase the microbial biomass, optimize the production of volatile fatty acids, reduce methane production and the risk of bloat, and stabilize the pH, diminishing the risk of acidosis. This product also contains

Oatinol TN, a natural source of antioxidants and polar lipids, to maintain gut-membrane health and function. It contains Natuphos 5000 G providing 500 FTU/kg of phytase activity.

Protein	18%
Oil	6%
Fibre	6%
Ash	10%
Lysine	1.1%
Vitamin A	7,000iu/kg
Vitamin D3	1,000iu/kg
Vitamin E (alpha tocopherol – added)	225iu/kg
Copper (cupric sulphate – added)	200mg/kg
Selenium (sodium selenite – added)	2mg/kg

Once again, this is a palatable feed, and unrestricted access to the bin can result in individuals overeating. The high inclusion rate of vitamins and minerals could then cause over dosage and toxicity.

Alfalfa / Lucerne Chaff

This is a useful supplemental feed in llamas and alpacas. It is not exactly forage, because it is chopped, and it has a relatively high protein, energy and mineral content:

Alfalfa Analysis (Dry Matter 92%)	
Metabolizable Energy	92 (MJ/kg DM)
Protein	8.2 (% DM)
Ash	2%
Oil	3.2%
Sugar	5.2%
Calcium	1.37%
Phosphorus	0.29%
Magnesium	0.21%
Potassium	1.9%
Sodium	0.14%
Sulphur	0.35%
Cobalt	0.28mg/kg
Copper	6.9mg/kg
Iodine	0.49mg/kg
Iron	145mg/kg
Manganese	25.4mg/kg

Molybdenum	1mg/kg
Zinc	22.4mg/kg
Selenium	0.14mg/kg
Vitamin E	34iu/kg
Beta-carotene	31.2mg/kg

Mole Valley Farmers Alpaca Winter Pellets

Oil	3%
Protein	18%
Fibre	9%
Ash	8.8%
Vitamin A	9,000iu/kg
Vitamin D3	1,800iu/kg
Vitamin E (alpha tocopherol)	100iu/kg
Selenium (sodium selenite)	0.6mg/kg
Copper (cupric sulphate)	50mg/kg

Charnwood Feeds

This East Anglian company will formulate customized rations if a sufficiently large order can be placed. It is currently working with a large local alpaca breeder in the area to establish the most appropriate formula.

Unless you are a qualified nutritionist, the analyses provided above will seem quite daunting. Some of the minerals, such as copper, cobalt, magnesium, zinc and selenium, have been associated with deficiency disease reported in the UK. You can compare the inclusion rates in the analyses. Part of your research for your llama or alpaca enterprise must include finding out what successful people in your area are feeding. Sadly, there are no hard and fast rules, because the nutritional content of forage varies from one area to another, and one pasture to another.

FEEDING METHODS

The method of providing feed for your animals is important. Because they are kept in groups, social hierarchies do – and should – develop. This means that there will be a boss animal in a group, and it will be allowed to take whatever it wants. As the lead animal, if it moves away from the feeding area once satisfied, the others will be inclined to follow, so

Alpacas on the altiplano in Peru, where feeding space is at less of a premium. (Photo: John Gaye, Alpacas of Wessex)

even if the dominant animal(s) have not consumed all of the food, the others are likely to follow them away and not eat it themselves. The result of these social pressures can be that the dominant animals are overfed and the sub-dominant ones fail to get enough.

The answer to the dilemma is space. The personal space of a feeding alpaca is about 3m (10ft). For a llama, add another 1m (3ft). If you ensure that each portion of food is separated from the next by about that distance, then even if the bossy animals move from one to another, the sub-dominant ones can swap portions and continue eating. If all the food is too close together, some animals will not get any. The more palatable the feed, the less likely it is that animals will wish to share a feeding station with each other, and I recommend that even forage stations are placed well apart, and enough of them provided so that each animal can have one to itself. How you do this depends on how many animals there are in your groups, and your equipment. I have seen individual bowls or buckets and long troughs used for milled feed, and racks, nets and bags used for hay and haylage.

A selection of feeding vessels. Having a number of different feeding stations minimizes the risk of low-ranking animals being bullied away from the food. In general, camelids prefer not to have to put their entire heads in a feeding vessel (thereby interfering with their sight) because they take their status as prey animals very seriously. (See Chapter 6.)

Hay Bags

These are simply old plastic feed bags clipped over a fence, with holes cut into them to allow the animals to pull the hay out. Their advantage is that they protect the hay from rain and oxidation and keep it palatable for three to four days, cutting wastage. Their disadvantage is that for large numbers of animals they are laborious to have to fill (although easier than nets) and that the animals marginally prefer to feed from nets. However, unless nets and racks are under cover, rain will spoil the forage within hours.

Introducing New Foods

Llamas and alpacas will be suspicious of unfamiliar things, and some individuals, especially young animals, will be quite reluctant to try an unfamiliar food. Often youngsters have been spat at when trying to sample adults' feed, and effectively 'trained' not to attempt to have any. It can take time and cunning to overcome this diffidence.

Most llamas and alpacas will find carrots and apples delicious. Many of them will also

A well-designed hayrack, which prevents the animals from raising their heads and adopting the posture of threatening display. This in turn discourages the intimidation of lower ranking animals.

A roofed hayrack, which will delay spoilage of hay by rain. Hayracks should be low and have troughs below them to minimize the amount of hay likely to fall out of the rack and contaminate fleece when animals lie on it. (Photo: Jean Field, Devon Alpacas)

eagerly eat other fruits and cabbage leaves, onion tops and so on. If you can scatter some chopped windfall apples or one of these other treats out in the pasture, so that even the youngsters get a chance to develop a taste for them, you can then use that food to tempt them to put their heads into the feed-trays or troughs. It is essential that there are enough feeding stations for them to have at least one each, or the bigger or bossier animals won't give them a look in. Some animals will feed peaceably together, but if the food is very appetizing, that is by no means guaranteed.

Watch Them Eat

Plan to allow yourself time to watch your group feed occasionally. It is only in observing the behaviour of the individuals and their feeding patterns and habits that you can fine-tune your methods to suit them. If the thinnest animal is a slow or shy feeder, consider trying to provide its meal separately, perhaps by feeding it in your yard. These animals are intelligent and will soon realize that you are helping them to get their share.
(Ref. C.N. Evans DVM, Notes for Proceedings of BAS International Conference 2000.)

CHAPTER 5

Husbandry

It is necessary regularly to perform certain maintenance procedures on your animals to keep them healthy and comfortable. Animals that are trained to accept handling, and that trust people, are far easier to treat than those that are not, and it is important when considering purchasing animals to decide how you intend to administer these routine treatments.

In addition to usual stable equipment, such as a shovel, a broom, buckets and haynets or bags, you will need halters and lead ropes. A variety of other equipment is available, but only from specialist sources. Some suppliers advertise in the camelid press. *See also* Useful Addresses.

THE FLEECE

Grooming

Alpacas
Alpacas are usually not groomed at all. This is because the natural growth of the fleece produces tiny waves (crimp) in huacaya animals, and twisting ringlets (locks) in suri animals. Grooming pulls these natural waves out, and interferes with the assessment of the quality of the fleece. Once-yearly shearing removes any matted tangled fleece, which is then skirted off the top-quality fibre and discarded or used in the production of low-quality items. Fortunately for most individuals, the fleece is

A selection of llama grooming tools. From left, a horse rubber currycomb, a plastic currycomb, two dog-style slicker brushes, a cushioned slicker brush, and a mat-splitter. The most effective of these is the cushioned slicker brush, which the animals accept fairly readily. The mat-splitter has very sharp blades to cut into mats, but tugs the coat and tends to cause the animal to object.

sufficiently thick to repel ordinary dirt, which falls off.

Llamas

Llamas usually require a degree of grooming to keep the surface of the fleece free of tangles and vegetable matter. A coarse 'slicker' brush is the most usual implement.

When a llama is groomed, the objective is to clear only the upper layer of the fleece of debris and tangles. It is neither desirable nor really possible to comb or brush down to skin level. The crossing of the fibres produces a degree of matting, which means that the animal would find the process very uncomfortable and it is unlikely to tolerate it for long.

The amount of grooming required depends on the type of fleece and where the animal is kept. Grassy pastures with lots of space and a good breeze keep fleeces cleaner than, for example, yards with straw or chippings down, or small enclosures with hedgerow borders containing brambles and burrs. In such cases, grooming may need to be carried out daily, or every two to three days.

In addition to keeping the coat comfortable and free from matted debris, grooming is a common way to harvest llama fibre. It has the advantage of leaving much of the coarse guard hair behind, yielding softer undercoat for processing. For coarser, harder-wearing products, where the guard hair is an advantage, shearing is a better method of harvesting fleece.

Shearing

This is normally performed annually. The best time to shear is the late spring because the animal should not need its fleece for warmth by then, and the grasses should not have flowered, so there will be minimal vegetable contamination of the fibre. For animals that are to be shown in summer shows, shearing is usually delayed as it is customary to show them in fleece.

Overheating in fully fleeced animals in summer can cause temporary infertility in stud male animals. The situation in females

> ### Tangles
>
> Paddocks containing plants that tend to tangle in fleeces should be avoided, and pasture management should be employed to stop plants like burdocks and ryegrasses coming to seed. There are many such plants whose seedpods tangle inextricably into fleece, and once this has happened the only option is to cut them out. Brambles frequently grow in hedgerows and are readily browsed by llamas and alpacas (they love blackberries!). When pieces of bramble become caught in fleeces they should be removed immediately. If left they can become embedded in the fleece and even begin to damage and break the skin. If tangled around the breech they can interfere with urination and defecation, causing matting of fibre with urine and faeces. This can in turn lead to fly-strike (infestation of the animal with blowfly maggots).

is less clear, but appetite tends to improve after shearing. At the very least a fully fleeced animal should have a cool shady retreat in summer. They will enjoy getting into water (and some may attempt, and succeed in, getting into the water trough) but muddy water and prolonged wetting will damage fleece. If the reason for not having shorn them is to enable you to show them, you want to avoid this happening.

If the fleece is not to be discarded, it should be dry when shorn. Therefore, if the weather is wet the animals must have been under cover for long enough to dry off, and shearing itself cannot take place in the open if it is raining. Wet or damp fleece will heat and rot if stored, and most fleece has to be stored before it is processed.

It is possible to shear a trained animal with hand-shears, while standing. However, this is a very laborious process, and leaves the animal looking rather moth-eaten. It is also difficult to retrieve the fleece in a single mass, making grading and skirting a long and piecemeal affair. If you are relieving single animals of fleece mainly for welfare reasons, hand-shearing is suitable, but most are shorn by a trained shearer using mechanical, electrically driven shears, like sheep shears. Special combs are used to cope with the different fibre characteristics of llamas and alpacas.

It is usual to restrain the llama or alpaca on its side for shearing, with the forelegs tied forwards, the hind legs backwards. This prevents it from struggling and rolling, and also gives the shearer the longest straight 'blows' possible, making the process faster and therefore less stressful for the animal. This also harvests the greatest possible amount of fibre without second cuts, which are short bits of wool left behind after the first cut. The

shearer takes them off to give a tidier appearance to the animal, but they are useless for processing, and therefore reduce the yield of top-grade fibre.

There are specially designed and constructed shearing tables, to which the animal is attached while standing, and then the whole table is rotated through 90 degrees so that the animal is lying on its side at the shearer's waist height. It is also common to lay the animal on the ground, tying the legs forwards and backwards, as described above, on top of a clean tarpaulin. Shearing at ground level is more taxing for the shearer, but obviously a cheaper and more portable option.

The animal is laid on the sheet and its legs tied in extension to restrain it in such a way that the shearer can safely cut the fleece away. (Photo: John Gaye, Alpacas of Wessex)

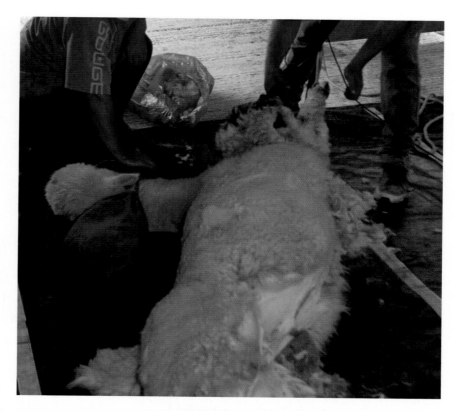

Note sandbags used to keep the head of the animal on the floor and to discourage struggling. The coarse fibre is being shorn from the legs first. (Photo: John Gaye, Alpacas of Wessex)

The assistant helps to steady the animal. (Photo: John Gaye. Alpacas of Wessex)

The assistant removes the coarser fibre to ensure that it does not become mixed with the premium fibre (to be shorn later). (Photo: John Gaye, Alpacas of Wessex)

The long blow down the back of the animal. Note that the shearer is now aiming to keep the premium blanket fibre all together, and to minimize the number of second cuts, which waste fibre. (Photo: John Gaye, Alpacas of Wessex)

The assistant collects a fibre sample for laboratory analysis. (Photo: John Gaye, Alpacas of Wessex)

Note the loosely woven bag over the animal's nose: this discourages both screaming and spitting. Many animals accept shearing with minimal complaint, but some scream in anger and protest, and spit as well. (Photo: John Gaye, Alpacas of Wessex)

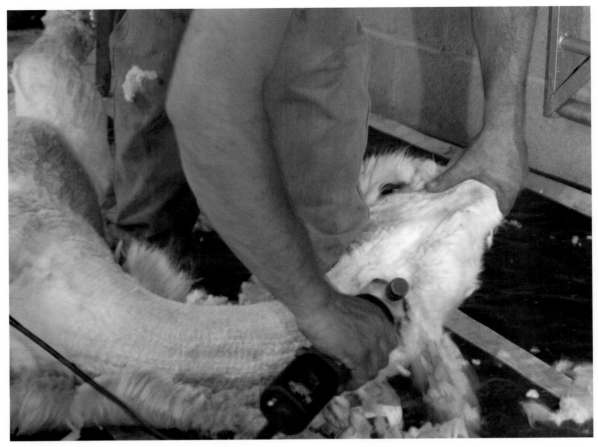

The shearing process is finished off with the head. (Photo: John Gaye, Alpacas of Wessex)

Some shearers will shear alpacas in the same way as sheep – with the animal sitting on its bottom – but this would not be practical for llamas.

RESTRAINT

For most of the maintenance procedures that have to be performed, some form of restraint is necessary. Alpacas can usually be manually restrained by a sufficiently commanding, strong person or persons, but llamas are too big for this. Many llamas are sufficiently well trained to stand once haltered and tied (and all should be); for those that are not, as a last resort a vet will usually be able to tranquilize or sedate the animal, although it will have to

be held still at least momentarily to do this. Sedation or even anaesthetic may also be used for those procedures that are unpleasant but unavoidable. The drugs frequently used for this purpose are xylazine, torbutrol, and ketamine, usually in some combination.

Restraint Chutes

If you intend handling large numbers of untrained animals, you will need a restraint chute. There are many designs of chute (*see* Chapter 3, page 32, for a simple design), but the important features are that the chute is solid (i.e., will not collapse if an animal throws itself against it), has rails, sides and gates placed to avoid trapping legs, and has anchorage points for restraint tapes or ropes.

It must also be built in a location in the yard that will make running the animals into it easy; the animals need to be able to run in one end and out the other.

Llamas and alpacas will frequently kush, or lie down on their chests, if they are convinced that something bad is going to happen and resistance is useless. A chute must take account of this tendency by having attachment points for restraining tapes so they can be held up, or provide enough space for tying them in this position so that they cannot get up until the procedure is finished. The gap between the sides and ground must not be such that legs can slip through and become trapped.

CASTRATION

Males that are unsuitable for breeding can make useful pet, working, fleece or companion animals. Castration makes them a little more tractable and prevents unwanted accidental pregnancies from genetically inferior individuals.

It is inadvisable to castrate a male before the age of eighteen months because in some individuals castration delays the cessation of growth, and they can become excessively tall and rangy. The exception to this general rule is the case of the so-called 'berserk male' (*see* Chapter 6), which should be castrated in the first year of life.

General anaesthesia is recommended for castration, although some veterinarians are able successfully to carry it out in the standing sedated animal. It is more cost-effective not to use general anaesthesia, but if the standing animal decides to kush the operation site will make contact with the ground, contaminating the wound and possibly causing infection and post-operative complications.

FEET

The feet of llamas and alpacas are not hooves (*see* photograph below). However, the large horny nails on the ends of their toes do commonly grow faster than they can be worn

The foot of a llama. Camelid feet have no hooves, but instead two soft digital pads, which spread as they take the animal's weight. The pads terminate in a pair of tough, horny nails, which have to be trimmed. (Photo: Chris Eke, UK Llamas)

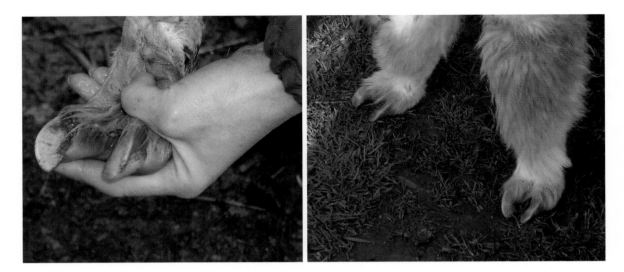

Overgrown feet. Note the nail twisting under the toe in the photograph on the left. If feet in this condition are not attended to, the nails will continue to grow and to curl, distorting the whole toe. (Photo: Tom Chamberlain)

down. When this happens they distort the way in which the foot contacts the ground, often causing the toes to twist over to one side. If left in this state, severe distortion of the foot can occur, and walking will eventu-ally become uncomfortable. Occasionally, espe-cially if the animal is kept on stony ground, the nails will break off altogether, although this, fortunately, rarely causes the animal a serious problem. Camelid feet are evolved to

Neatly trimmed feet provide a level bearing surface for the animal. (Photo: Tom Chamberlain)

The blade of the foot clipper must be gently and firmly inserted between the pad and the nail to trim away the curling, ingrowing horn from the sides.

The overlong tip of the nail is trimmed straight off, taking care to avoid cutting too much off, which would cause the toe to bleed.

deal with arid conditions, which tend to produce hard, abrasive ground. In the UK, the wet climate means that the ground is frequently too soft to wear the toenails down. In periods of persistently damp conditions, toenails can require trimming once a month; if the weather has been drier, every six to nine weeks may be sufficient. Working llamas tend to wear the toenails down naturally and require less trimming.

If toenails are not kept trimmed, they and the toes can become permanently distorted, and cease to grow straight, increasing the problems they cause when they get too long, and also causing loss of marks for conformation in the show or sale ring. Permanent damage to the joints of the foot and legs can also result. If the feet have become twisted, frequent trimming encourages them to recover a straighter growth because weight bearing while the nails are short helps to pull them straight. Get into the habit of checking the animals' feet as you feed and handle them.

Technique

Toenails can be trimmed with sheep or lamb foot-shears. The operation is slightly easier when the feet have been on moist ground; the nails get harder as they dry out. The objective is to shorten them as far as possible without cutting the sensitive tissues, so as to promote a level bearing surface for the foot and straight nail growth in future.

Ideally the animal will have been trained to stand while each foot is raised, so that the operator can lift the foot from the ground and hold it in one hand while trimming with the other. If the animal is not trained, it must be restrained by an assistant. Alarmed animals may well struggle and even kush when their feet are handled.

Once the foot is turned over, with the sole facing upward, use the tip of the trimmers to clean out any dirt or mud, so that the length of free nail can be distinguished from the sole. If the nail is not so long that flattening its V-shaped profile will cause discomfort, then cut across the tip, back to the level of the sole, leaving enough horn to keep the sensitive tissues covered. Then make two more cuts down each side of the V to bring the whole nail level with the sole. If there is twisting of the toe, attempt to trim back any nail lying around the toe.

TEETH

Adult llamas and alpacas have twenty-eight to thirty-two permanent teeth. These consist of incisors, canines, premolars, and molars. The deciduous (milk) teeth number only eighteen to twenty-two and do not include molars. (*See* box opposite.) Unusually for cud-chewing grazers, they do have an upper incisor. However, this tooth has moved back to the side of the jaw and evolved into a

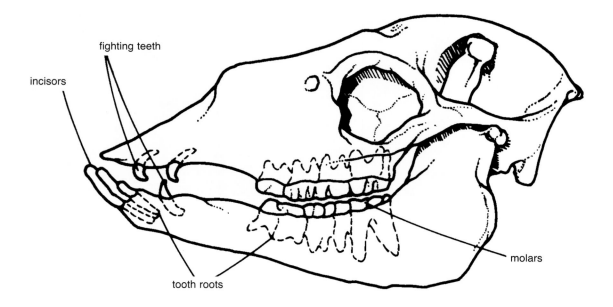

Diagram of camelid skull showing teeth and approximate positions of teeth roots. Note particularly the fighting teeth, which must be kept trimmed in entire male animals.

fighting tooth, joining the upper and lower canines in that function.

Teeth Trimming

The natural diet of llamas and alpacas is high in silicates, which cause plants to be tough and abrasive to eat. These animals' teeth are therefore steadily extruded through the gums throughout life in the expectation that chewing this tough forage will gradually wear them away. In the UK, where forage is softer, it is relatively common to find that the teeth appear faster than they are worn down. As a result they can become overlong, especially in the case of incisors.

When the animal grazes, it must clamp the grass between the incisor teeth on its bottom jaw and the dental pad on the upper jaw (there are no functional upper incisors – the upper incisors have evolved into fighting teeth), so that a quick flick of the muzzle cuts

Dentition

Following are the dental formulas for permanent and deciduous teeth in llamas and alpacas. The numbers refer to only one side of the mouth, so they should be doubled to give the total.

Permanent teeth: incisors 1/3; canines 1/1; premolars 1–2/1–2; molars 3/3

Deciduous teeth: incisors 1/3; canines 1/1; premolars 2–3/1–2; molars 0/0.

Fighting teeth develop in all males and in some females. (The upper incisors and the canines are adapted to become fighting teeth.) They appear in the space on the gums between the molars and the incisors. They are present on both the upper jaw (which has two on each side), and on the lower (which has one on each side), and they are directed backward so that they can be used for ripping opponents. Fighting teeth are capable of inflicting serious, even fatal, injury during fights so they should be trimmed to 1–2mm length from the gum.

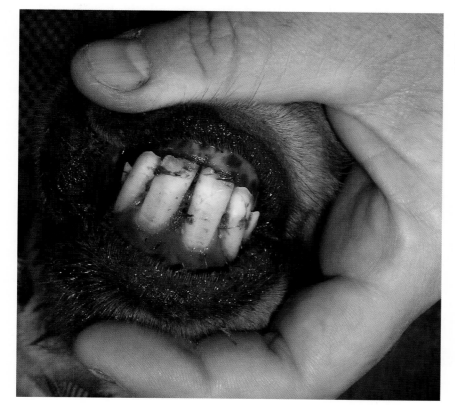

Overgrown teeth. The incisors completely obscure the dental pad. (Photo: Tom Chamberlain)

the grass off. Therefore, if the incisors cannot be brought into contact with the dental pad, grazing becomes less efficient. It is accepted that if when you part the lips of the animal there is a gap of more than a couple of millimetres between the front of the dental pad and the back of the teeth, then the teeth should be trimmed back.

In the show or sale ring, failure of occlusion of the incisors (i.e. failure of the incisors to contact the dental pad) is a reason to reduce the value of the animal, since poor digestion from failure to bite or chew effectively, or problems in the mouth from rubbing of out-of-line teeth, become more likely. (*See* Chapter 9.) The more serious fault is failure of the incisors to reach forward far enough to a position opposite the dental pad. This occurs because the bottom jaw is too short, so no amount of tooth trimming will ever overcome the problem because it cannot make the jaw longer. Teeth that protrude from the front of the lips and overshoot the dental pad can at least be trimmed to the correct length.

Trimming teeth is not an easy procedure, since using hand-held clippers of any sort will cause teeth to shatter and splinter, so it

Ear tag pliers. The tag is correctly loaded, ready for insertion.

must be done with a mechanical grinding tool, commonly an angle-grinder or Dremel tool. Usually a piece of plastic pipe or similar is used as a gag to keep the lips safely out of the way. The animals dislike the procedure, and it is most often performed at the same time as shearing, when they are cast on the ground and tied.

It is usual for shearers to offer incisor trimming as part of their service, and also usual for them to charge extra for each animal that they do it on. This provides them with an incentive to find more animals who 'need' the procedure, and owners must be vigilant to prevent over-zealous trimming of normal mouths. There is no benefit to trimming a normal mouth; on the contrary, you risk cutting and distressing an animal to no purpose.

It is possible that maintaining an ideal bite with the incisors will help the cheek teeth to remain properly aligned and reduce any tendency to fail to meet. Problems with cheek teeth are much more difficult to solve because access to the back of the mouth is difficult.

EAR TAGGING

Identification ear tags are usually inserted when crias are just a few days or weeks old. Usually females have tags in the left ear, and males in the right. There are several different designs of tag, and each has specially designed pliers for insertion. A hole is punched through the ear and the tag threaded through it. Surprisingly, the animals do not object much to this.

It is important when applying ear tags to ensure cleanliness. Do not leave the tags or pliers lying around in a dirty place. Any part of the equipment that contacts the ear should be thoroughly cleaned after use and before the next use. The tags should be kept in their packs until the last possible moment before application. These precautions will minimize the chances of the punched hole becoming infected.

The operator should positively identify the blood vessels that run along the ear and

Ear tagging, step 1. Locate the space between the tendinous ridges in the ear with your fingers. The tag makes its own hole. Larger flag tags and button tags are also used.

Ear tagging, step 2. Crunch the pliers firmly together to insert the tag. A swift, firm action will cause less pain than a tentative gradual one. Grit your teeth if you need to.

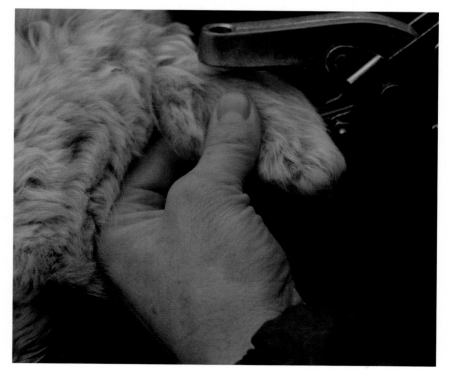

*Ear tagging, step 3.
Rotate the tag to check
that it moves freely in its
hole and that no tag of
skin remains attached to
it. If you have chosen
your site well, it will
not bleed.*

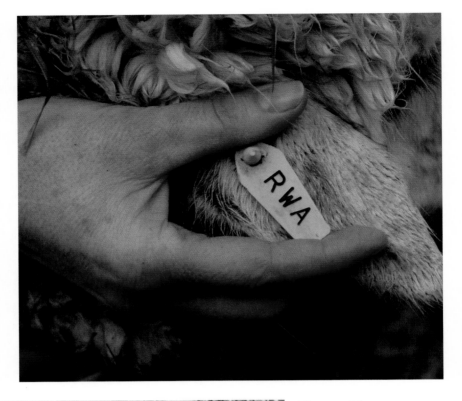

*Flag tag. These are
more convenient to
read from a distance,
but are also more
likely to get caught or
pulled out. (Photo:
Karen Oglesby, Meon
Valley Alpacas)*

The usual site for the insertion of a microchip. This is the site favoured in the UK. Bear in mind that with imported animals other sites may have been used, including other sites in the neck, the body and tail folds. An animal should always be scanned all over its body before it is assumed to have no chip.

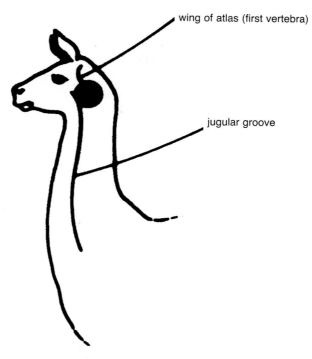

wing of atlas (first vertebra)

jugular groove

avoid them with the punch. When inserting tags it is important to ensure that the tag rotates freely and has not trapped the edge of the skin. The photographs on pages 59–60 illustrate the correct procedure.

MICROCHIPPING

Almost all llamas and alpacas in the UK are permanently and uniquely identified by a microchip, which is implanted beneath the skin. This tiny, rice-grain-sized bead can be read by a scanner and will show the unique identifying number of the chip on the scanner's screen. The usual site for the implantation of microchips in the UK is about 10cm (4in) below the left ear; in many imported animals, microchips may be found in various sites, including the base of the neck, and the tail fold. If a chip is not found when the usual implantation site is scanned, it is a good idea to scan the whole body of the animal to check

Microchip in its packing (right) together with implanter (left). The chip itself nestles within the insertion needle in the pack, and is about the size of a grain of rice.

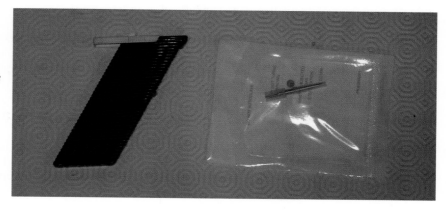

that it has not either been inserted elsewhere or migrated.

Implantation of Microchips

The technique is basically the same as for a subcutaneous injection – by pulling up a tent of skin and placing the chip beneath it. But it is not possible to draw back to ensure that the needle tip is not in a blood vessel or out of the skin altogether. For this reason, the site must be selected to avoid any vital structures, and it is better to have microchips implanted by an experienced operator, or get one to show you how to do it.

As with injections, cleanliness is essential. It is very much easier to be sure that it is correctly implanted in the short-fleeced animal, since long fleece makes it difficult to see what you are doing. My technique is to locate by feel the bony ridge of the wing of the atlas vertebra (*see* diagram on page 61) and also the jugular groove. I aim to insert the chip a little further from the head than the wing of the atlas, and above the jugular groove, to avoid the blood vessels and nerves that run there. Once the chip has been implanted, the animal should be scanned to confirm that the chip is in place.

VACCINATIONS

It is usual to vaccinate llamas and alpacas against Clostridial diseases, using vaccines licensed for use in sheep and cattle. (There are no vaccines specifically licensed for llamas or alpacas.) At the time of writing there are no data on the ability of these vaccines to produce a protective immunity, but since the diseases concerned are fatal, and the vaccines relatively cheap and apparently relatively safe, we do it in the hope that they are beneficial. The diseases themselves tend to be sporadic (*see* Chapter 13) so it is very difficult to know whether or not the vaccines help us.

There are up to ten Clostridial diseases that affect domestic livestock, although not all or them have been reported in llamas and

One of the anti-Clostridial vaccines used in llamas and alpacas. Others have also been used, and recommendations change from time to time. Keep in contact with your veterinary surgeon regarding current practice.

alpacas. The vaccinations usually contain between four and ten of the diseases in an inactivated form. To help stimulate the immune system, irritant substances are added to the vaccine, and these can cause localized swelling or occasionally more severe reactions. It is thought that without some degree of local reaction, the vaccine is probably less effective.

Vaccine Regimes

Various regimes for vaccination have been tried and are recommended by different authorities. However, the following principles are generally agreed:

- Animals should not be vaccinated around the time of conception or in early pregnancy. At these times any disturbance or toxicity is more likely to cause foetal abnormality or loss.
- At least two vaccinations will be required in any one animal to produce a protective immunity. Typically these will be given one month apart.

- Booster injections should be given at least annually.

I do not wish to give definitive vaccine advice here. The incidence of disease varies with locality, and recommendations change fairly often, as do the preparations available. It is important to consult your local camelid veterinarian to ascertain what is regarded as best practice in your particular area at any one time. Clostridial diseases are sporadic in nature, so even in an unprotected herd they may crop up only now and then. Conversely, Clostridial disease has been reported in vaccinated animals as well.

VITAMIN INJECTIONS

The UK is at fairly high latitude, so in the winter the days become very short. Llamas and alpacas have evolved at low latitudes where at all times of year there are long hours of daylight, and bright dry skies, too. The UK's gloomy, short winter days will provide insufficient sunlight for the production of Vitamin D in the skin, especially in growing animals. It is therefore good practice to supplement Vitamin D by injecting it three or four times during each winter. As a rough guide, plan to administer Vitamin D every six weeks between the autumn and spring equinoxes.

WORMING

Internal parasites have part of their life cycle outside the primary mammal host, so exposure to them depends on a number of local factors. You need to make local enquiries as to which parasites are seen in your area, and then plan for controlling those. (*See* Chapter 13.) The usual practice with farmed animals is to use wormers only when the need arises rather than as a matter of course. This is to reduce the probability of the development of resistance to worming drugs.

Usually the problem times for worms are: the early summer (for this season's crias), the early autumn (when worms try to go dormant in the host for the winter), and late winter (when dormant worms are starting to emerge). However, since UK summers can be cold and wet, and the winters mild, these danger times can slip in either direction. There are no hard and fast dates but, if parasites are found to be present in your animals and on the ground, be prepared to worm at least three times per year.

Some wormers are administered by injection. I usually find that llamas and alpacas do not object unduly to these, but if they are not halter-trained and accustomed to handling, restraint is necessary.

INJECTION TECHNIQUE

If you are going to administer your own injections – wormers, vitamins, and so on – get a veterinary surgeon to demonstrate the technique and coach you in it before you attempt it. These notes are for guidance to remind you of the technique, but trying to learn it from a book alone will be difficult.

There are two routes of injection usable by laypersons. These are subcutaneous (also abbreviated to S/C, sub Q, or S/Q), meaning under the skin, and intramuscular (abbreviated to I/M) and meaning into the muscle ('into the muscular', as my sister used to say when we were children on the farm).

The main difference between the two routes is in the speed of the uptake of the injected substance. The blood supply to the muscles is greater than that of the subcutaneous site, and injected substances are therefore dispersed more rapidly. Since the blood supply to the tissues beneath the skin is less good, substances will be absorbed more slowly. However, the advantage of the subcutaneous site is that it is more comfortable for the animal so, if time is not critical, the subcutaneous route may be preferable. For injections where a rapid uptake is required the I/M site is preferable. The I/M site may also be recommended if the substance is potentially irritant: if injected into the muscle it will not remain *in situ* for long enough to create tissue damage; under the skin it could create an ulcer by causing the overlying skin to be destroyed. The disadvantage of the intramuscular route is that it is more uncomfortable for the animal, and therefore more likely to make it start or object.

There are researchers in America who maintain that all routine injections in camelids can be given by the subcutaneous route, and that local reactions to them do not seem to be a problem and nor does uptake from the tissues beneath the skin.

The diagrams on this page show recommended sites for injection. The reason for

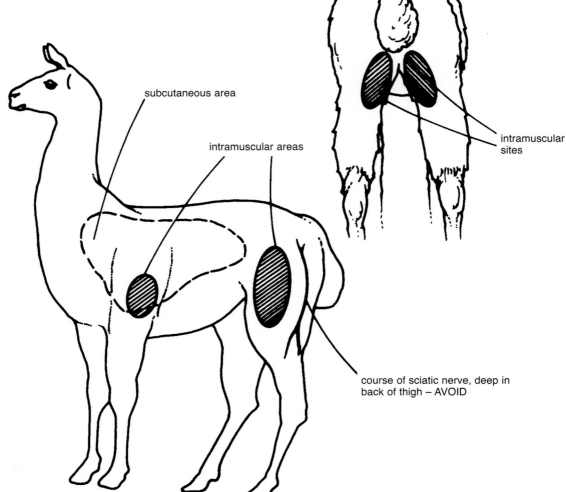

subcutaneous area

intramuscular areas

intramuscular sites

course of sciatic nerve, deep in back of thigh – AVOID

Injection sites.

confining injections to the suggested sites is that in these places you are least likely accidentally to puncture some vital structure should you slip or should the animal jump during the procedure.

Procedure

Filling the Syringe

1. Use a single-use disposable syringe, with a new unused needle. These things cost pennies, and it is simply not worth risking infections by using dirty technique and equipment.

2. Open the packing of the syringe and handle it by the barrel: avoid touching the luer tip with your fingers or any object. Then open the needle, avoiding touching the hub; handle the needle by the casing. Holding the needle by the casing, fit the hub over the luer tip of the syringe, and press home, while twisting to ensure a secure fit. You should have avoided touching the hub or the tip, so that the connection remains sterile.

3. Shake the bottle of medicine (if this is required), until properly suspended. If it is a new bottle, remove the protective metal seal from the centre of the rubber bung with a clean knife or scissors tip. This should leave a metal collar around the bung to hold it securely in the bottle. If the bottle is not new, swab the top with surgical spirit to ensure that it is clean.

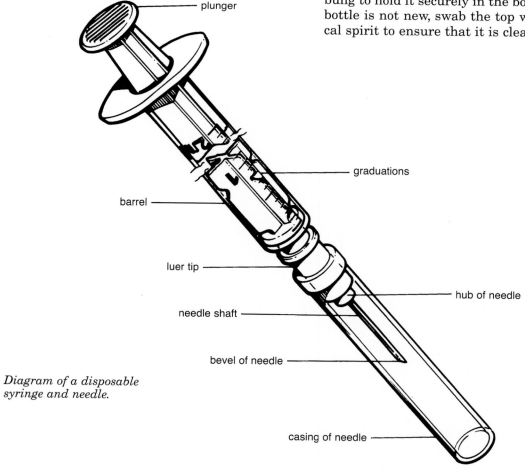

Diagram of a disposable syringe and needle.

plunger

graduations

barrel

luer tip

needle shaft

hub of needle

bevel of needle

casing of needle

4. Withdraw the plunger until you have drawn as much air into the syringe as you will need of medicine. Uncover the needle by sliding the plastic cover off it with a straight pull. (Do not twist, or the needle will come off the syringe.)

5. Push the needle through the rubber bung on the bottle, and depress the syringe plunger to force the dose of air into the bottle. The positive pressure you have created in the bottle will now help you to withdraw the medicine.

6. Keeping the needle in the bottle, turn it and the syringe upside down, so that the syringe is below the bung, and pointing upwards into the bottle. Now withdraw the plunger to fill the syringe with the correct amount of medicine. If air bubbles come into the syringe, flick the barrel of it gently to get them to the top of the chamber, and inject them back into the bottle. Then withdraw the plunger again to get the correct

dose, without any air bubbles. You may need to do this a couple of times with some medicines to eliminate all the air bubbles. (It's not that a tiny amount of clean injected air in the S/C or I/M sites will do any harm; it's just that air is not medicine and you will get the dose wrong.)

7. Hold the plunger steady as you turn the bottle up the right way again, and pull the syringe with needle attached out of the rubber bottle bung. Immediately cover the needle with its plastic casing again, both to keep it clean and to prevent accidentally scratching or pricking anyone. Remember that the needle cover slides straight on over the needle, and that the needle hub twists onto and off the luer tip of the syringe.

Administering the Injection

1. Select the injection site (*see* diagrams on page 64). It is important to ensure that the

Locate fold of skin by feeling through the fleece.

site is clean and that dirty fleece does not contaminate the needle tip. If there is a reasonable amount of fleece the skin will often be quite clean beneath it. If it is not, clean with surgical spirit.

2. Uncover the needle by pulling the plastic cover straight off. I usually just do a final twist and push together of the needle and syringe before doing this, to make sure that the needle hub is really secure on the syringe luer tip.

3. Handle the syringe by holding the barrel with your fingers; if you hold it by the plunger, you risk expelling the contents accidentally before you are ready.

The remainder of the procedure depends on the injection route chosen:

Subcutaneous injections
1. Part the fleece to expose clean skin. If you are right-handed, pinch up a tent of skin with the fingers of your left hand (vice versa if you are left-handed). Then aim the needle at right angles to the sloping roof of the tent so that the tip will be inside it. If you have pulled up a good enough tent, the needle will be nearly parallel to the rest of the animal.

2. Once the needle is under the skin, pull back on the plunger. It should resist. If you pull air into the syringe, then you have either failed to penetrate the skin, or you have gone straight through the tent and out the other side. Reposition the needle and try again.

3. If blood comes back into the chamber, you have accidentally punctured a vessel. Remove the needle and syringe, very carefully, and gently depress the plunger enough to expel any blood, but not any medicine, and reposition. Repeat the pulling back to check that you are in the correct place.

Pinch up a tent of skin, holding it firmly with finger tips. Insert needle into the tent.

Draw back on needle. There should be resistance to the backward movement of the plunger, and no blood should appear at the needle hub.

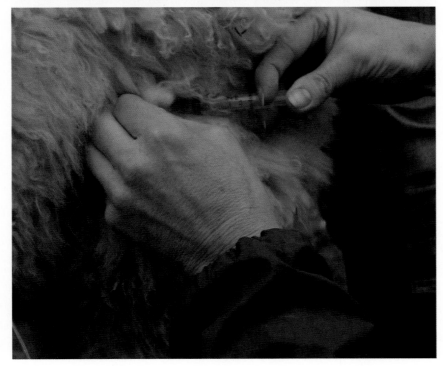

Inject by depressing plunger.

4. If you do not draw either air or blood into the syringe chamber, and instead get the typical resistance to movement of the plunger, it is safe to depress the syringe plunger and administer the injection.

Intramuscular injections:
1. Part the fleece to expose clean skin. Use the fingers of the left hand (vice versa if you are left-handed) to grip and stabilize the muscle mass while you insert the needle straight into the muscle. Hold the syringe by the barrel so that if the animal starts you do not accidentally inject before you are ready.
2. Pull back on the plunger to check that there is no blood coming into the syringe. (If there is, pull the needle and syringe out and reposition.) Administer the injection by depressing the plunger.

DRENCHING

Some wormers, anti-coccidials and vitamins are administered by drenching. There are many devices designed to drench domestic livestock, but for llamas and alpacas a large plastic syringe is tolerated as well as anything, and should be sufficient for all except large numbers of animals. (With large numbers, the rubber plunger will start to wear out with repeated use.) It is not necessary to use a new sterile syringe for each drench dose. A standard drench 'gun' can also be used if large numbers are to be dosed.

For the drenching procedure it is sensible to have no one standing in front of the animal as it is perhaps the occasion when the animal is most likely to spit. For untrained adult animals a chute may be needed, but if the animal is trained it should be lightly restrained on the operator's left side (vice versa if the operator is left-handed). Often, holding the head still by gripping the ears in the left hand will produce sufficient steadiness. An assistant to hold the ears from the animal's left side, so that the operator can steady the muzzle and keep it elevated with the left hand, is helpful.

The mouth must be held above the level of the throat and neck, or the drench will run out. The nozzle of the drenching device (syringe or drench 'gun') should gently be introduced into the side of the mouth where there are no teeth, and directed to the inside of the cheek teeth, between the teeth and the tongue. Do not shove the nozzle too far down or the animal will panic. Depress the plunger or trigger slowly, to give the animal time to swallow the liquid, keeping the nose elevated above the throat. Listen and watch for swallowing. Keep the nose up until this has taken place, or the animal will spit the drench out.

WEANING

If you are breeding your animals, at some point you will have to undertake the heart-breaking task of separating the mums from their growing youngsters.

Why Wean?
If left to themselves, eventually the mothers would stop allowing their offspring to feed, but they will do this at variable times. In order for the female to catch up on her body reserves for next year's cria, she needs to have a few months off lactation. The other problem if you leave last year's cria in with her is that it may well still be feeding from its mother as she runs up to her next calving, and will take the colostrum, which is essential for the new baby. All in all, we wean for the sake of next year's cria, although with mothers who are not giving much milk the offspring frequently grow better after weaning, when they have to rely exclusively on concentrates and forage, because they can get as much of them as they want. Therefore, the weaned animals grow better too, as long as the nutrition is ideal.

How to Wean
Separating the mothers from their babies for a few weeks will allow the mother's udder to dry off. It is not usual to attempt any antibiotic or other treatment of the udder, mastitis

being rare in camelids. The back pressure of milk which is no longer being taken by the cria causes the gland to stop secreting, so it is usual for the glands to appear quite swollen with unconsumed milk for the first few days. This causes some discomfort to the mother, in addition to the distress she will feel at being separated from her baby, and she will often call for her cria. After about six weeks her udder should have reached the stage at which it will not start to produce milk again even if the cria is put back with her. However, if you do put the cria back, she may well allow it to attempt to feed, and when she produces colostrum for the next birth, it will be lost to a persistent yearling cria.

The mothers and crias should be separated so that they cannot see or hear each other. The crias will try to crawl, wriggle or push their way out of the enclosure into which they are put, but especially so when their mothers are in view or can be heard. For this reason the fencing needs to be secure, and such that they will not damage themselves when they try to get out – for try they surely will. The mothers are usually less frantic, but will call to the babies if they can see or hear them. Attempts by the crias to escape are more determined (and therefore more likely to cause injury) if they can see their mothers.

While mothers and crias should be seperated, they should nevertheless be in groups: no animal should ever be left alone. It is comforting for the crias to have an unrelated mature animal with them, such as a gelding, or an older female who has no baby. It is theoretically possible for male crias to become fertile at nine months of age, so plan to separate male from female before this time. Even if they are not fertile, their enthusiastic attempts to practise being stud males will pester the female crias, and the males will be more inclined to fight each other.

If you have a small herd, and also someone near by who also breeds camelids, you can cooperate over weaning so that no animal needs to be left alone, and you can get the mothers properly separated from the babies.

If you are going to do this, you must also discuss the biosecurity for each holding, as well as parasite management.

THE HUSBANDRY YEAR

Most husbandry tasks need to be repeated at certain times of the year. There follows here a summary of the tasks that apply to each season for most llamas and alpacas. Depending upon season, circumstances and individual factors, almost all of them may need to be performed in almost any month, but this is a rough guide to their usual occurrence.

January
- Condition score animals.
  At this time of year the animals will usually have fairly thick fleeces, so that it is difficult to see how fat or thin they are. Every time you condition score, you should expect to have an explanation for all animals not within a score of the ideal 3 out of a scale of 5, and take any action required.
- Check feet for toenail growth.
- Supplement with Vitamin D for growing (under three years old) pregnant or lactating animals.

February
- Condition score.
- Check feet.
- Worm any thin animals, which may have carried worms into winter.
- Plan weaning of any crias still on their mothers.
- Plan matings for later in the year, so that the stud males you want to use can be booked.
- Check sale dates for early entry of surplus animals.

March
- Condition score. Pay particular attention to females due to calve in the spring. Ensure that the nutrition of these animals is fully supplemented with vitamins and minerals.

- Check feet.
- Vitamin D injections for growing, pregnant and lactating animals.
- Wean crias that are still on their mothers unless their new crias are not due until late summer.
- Halter-train crias.
- Plan which sales and shows you wish to attend, and get entry forms.
- Vaccinate pregnant females as advised by your vet.

April
- Condition score.
- Check feet.
- Continue training crias for showing, loading, trekking, as appropriate.
- Decide on shearing date and make arrangements for shearing.
- Find clean pasture for any show animals.
- Prepare for arrival of this season's crias by arranging accommodation, and checking calving supplies. (*See* Chapter 12.)

May
- The first crias will be arriving. Attend to calving and nursery areas to ensure that no build up of disease agents can occur there.
- Check with your vet regarding vaccination of new crias.
- The show season is starting: ensure seed-free clean pasture for show animals.
- Condition score and check feet.
- Matings can begin if you wish to have April-born crias next year.
- Shearing can take place if it fits with calvings and showing.

June
- Condition score and check feet.
- The calving season continues.
- The show season continues.
- Matings and spit-offs take place.
- Ultrasound pregnancy scanning.
- Shearing can take place.
- Attend to pasture management to ensure worm-free grazing and Coccidia free calv-

ing areas. Depending upon weather, plan moving stock to clean pasture.
- Make hay if you have the land and the weather.

July
- Check condition scores. They should be at their best in all but lactating females.
- Do worm-egg counts including liver fluke if appropriate.
- Worm and vaccinate.
- Check feet.
- Be prepared to move animals to clean grazing if not done in June (this depends upon weather through the summer).
- Calving, mating, spitting off, showing.
- Ultrasound pregnancy scanning.
- Shear any animals that have been delayed for showing.
- Make hay if you have the land and the weather.

August
- Condition score and check feet.
- Attend shows.
- Mating and spitting off.
- Ultrasound pregnancy scanning.
- Assess worm/fluke status; treat if appropriate.
- Vaccinate/boost where appropriate for new crias.
- Ear tag and microchip new crias.

September
- Condition score and check feet.
- Calving of later crias.
- Attend to worm/fluke status where appropriate.
- Matings; spitting off.
- Ultrasound pregnancy scanning.
- Arrange hay or haylage for winter feed.
- Microchip and register new crias.

October
- Condition score and check feet.
- Last matings, spitting off and ultrasound scanning, depending upon how late you are willing to have your crias born.

The winter sunshine is too brief and weak to meet the Vitamin D requirements of llamas and alpacas in northern Europe.

- Start Vitamin D supplementation for youngstock.
- Treat for worms or fluke as appropriate, depending upon weather.
- Microchip and register new crias if not done last month.

November
- Condition score and check feet.
- Expect increased intake of hay as grass fails.
- Arrange for sheltered pasture as weather deteriorates.

- Supplement Vitamin D if not done last month.
- Ultrasound scanning to see which females are pregnant.

December
- Condition score and check feet.
- Ensure sufficient feeding stations for all animals to have access to good hay and water, as well as any concentrates that are fed.
- Supplement Vitamin D if not done last month.

CHAPTER 6

Behaviour, Handling and Training

It is very important to take account of the normal and instinctive behaviour of llamas and alpacas when handling and training them. Their basic psychological make-up has a major influence on the way they respond to human handling, and understanding it will make planning your interactions with them a much more rational exercise. Eric Hoffman has done much superb work on the behaviour of South American camelids, and I recommend his publications to readers who wish to know more on the subject. Many of the terms I have used in this chapter I encountered first in his work.

THE PREY ANIMAL

Llamas and alpacas, like most domestic livestock, are evolved and selectively bred from wild animals. In the wild, these animals are herbivorous, and form the food source for large predators. In the case of the South American camelids, the major predators are man and the lynx (a large cat).

Survival in the wild, and even of domestic populations that are ranched in extensive open ranges, depends on having highly developed defence reflexes, which will maximize the chances of detecting and escaping attack from predators. One of the most important defence mechanisms that they possess is their excellent sight, which means that they have a chance of detecting a predator, competitor or mate from a great distance. It is unusual to come upon a group of llamas or

alpacas without being detected by at least one individual very early in your approach. Some of their behaviour derives from the need to produce meaningful signals visible from a considerable distance, so that they can communicate with one another without wasting energy on approaching closely.

Llamas and alpacas use their sensitive hearing to help them to pinpoint the areas within their visual field that should be observed closely – for a predator, rival or mate.

This means that they are inherently shy animals – cautious, watchful, inclined to flee if threatened, and to struggle if caught, and that their first idea about a strange animal or person is that it is a life-threatening predator. Successful handling of them is therefore based on gaining their trust and confidence.

SOCIAL STRUCTURE

Llamas and alpacas are social animals, which expect to live in groups. The group will be ruled by a dominant individual who will guide it to food, shelter, and safety. In return, the other members of the group help with sentry duty, and yield up first rights to food, sex and any-

thing else it might want. The sub-dominant ones do not seem to resent this; on the contrary, they appear to feel safer when in the company of a powerful individual. They seem to have no concept of what we would call fairness, and accept the authority of the dominant animal.

The social group is the environment in which each individual learns how to interact with the others – to learn the 'Rules of the Game'. It is therefore important for young individuals to spend their formative months in a stable group of adults so that they can develop their social skills.

LANGUAGE

Voice

Llamas and alpacas have a number of voices. The most common is a slightly anxious-sounding 'mmmm' noise. They can also grunt, whine, cluck softly and even scream. They express defiant disapproval by spitting. If they wish only to warn, then often they will spit past or away from the other animal, but if they are really angry, they will spit directly at it. Spit is foul-smelling liquid from the C1 fermentation compartment of the stomach, and it seems to upset the spitter almost as much as it does the spittee. Often both animals will develop a droopy lower lip and lose interest in food for several minutes after the incident. Sub-dominant animals rarely dare to spit at the dominant one.

Ear Position

This is another key indicator of mood and forthcoming behaviour. Forward-positioned ears denote eagerness and curiosity. Laid-back ears denote fear, anger, alarm or submission, and are usually accompanied by a raised muzzle. This position always precedes spitting.

Tail Position

A tail slightly raised from the buttocks is an assertive status-confirming sign. Llamas normally carry their tails a little raised in this way when walking. Alpacas need to be more alarmed or excited to do it. If flipped over the back (in llamas or alpacas), it is submissive.

The grandeur of the landscape dwarfs the alpacas, which can just be discerned in the left lower half of the photograph, at the very foot of the mountains. The ability to communicate over distance with a minimum of energy expenditure is vital in this environment. (Photo: John Gaye, Alpacas of Wessex)

These youngsters are quite happy to huddle together for warmth and company on a cold night. When they get older, they will expect more individual space each, and sub-dominant individuals may be excluded from a shelter that is small or with a narrow entrance. (Photo: Chris Eke, UK Llamas)

Some ear and head positions in llamas. Ear positions denote attentiveness, interest, alarm or aggression. Head positions denote status within the group.

Tail raised and curved away from buttocks. This is the stance of the alert, interested, unthreatened animal.

Tail flipped over the back. This denotes complete submission and lack of resistance.

The black female in the centre of the picture is demonstrating a typical warning-off posture, with flattened ears and raised muzzle – even though she hasn't yet troubled to rise. (Photo: Karen Oglesby, Meon Valley Alpacas)

These two individuals give each other a broadside display to assert dominance in a dispute over a vantage point. (Photo: Chris Eke, UK Llamas)

Broadside Displays

These are employed by males to indicate that the individual concerned considers himself master of the territory, and will repel any encroaching male. The animal presents himself side-on, to allow his full size and splendour to be perceived, and elevates his tail slightly so that it stands out from his buttocks, increasing his apparent size. At the same time the ears are laid back in a clear unwelcoming signal, the muzzle is elevated, and the lips drawn from the teeth in an aggressive mouth-open snarl, possibly to show off fighting fangs and readiness to use them. Females can use broadside displays to amorous males if they are intending to reject attempts to mate.

The Stand-Off Position

This involves two or more animals that have not yet reached agreement about which is dominant. They position themselves inside each other's personal space (i.e. within neck reach) and both (or all, if more than two) stand rigidly with head and tail raised, ears back, muzzle raised, in readiness for spitting, screeching or biting, any of which may ensue if one does not back down. In a stable group, these stand-offs are relatively rare; they denote doubt about the pecking order. If they are frequent, it implies that the group is being stressed in some way, often by a lack of resources such as space, feeding areas, shelter, shade or water.

Submissive Crouch

This posture is most often used by an immature individual, typically a cria or weanling. It signals lack of aggression or presumption, and assures the other individual that no threat is offered. The first thing the submissive animal does is to raise its tail right over its back, flipping it along the spine. If more assurance seems to be required, the head is lowered, and the front legs flexed slightly. The ears are directed back, out of harm's way.

If this position is being seen often in a particular individual within its group then it suggests that it is being bullied. This situation is likely to be associated with reduced opportunities to feed, drink or have access to shelter or shade if space is at all limited.

Kicking

To a llama or alpaca this is a legitimate defensive action, and the animal will lash out if surprised and therefore alarmed by a light touch. It says, 'Oi, get away from me.' They can kick forwards as well as backwards. They very rarely use the front feet to strike.

Biting

Llamas and alpacas will, in extreme rage, bite each other. It is very rare for them to attempt to bite a human, except in the case of the so-called 'berserk male' or, as it is perhaps more correctly known, the imprinted animal (*see* page 80). Biting is a feature of fights between males, which is why fighting teeth are nor-

mally trimmed, since they can do considerable damage (*see* Chapter 5). It is common for fighting animals to bite at one another's front legs, neck or genitals.

Rearing

This is an aggressive action, used to dominate each other. Youngsters will do it in play, but adults in earnest are attempting to subdue the other animal by rising above it and coming down on top of it. Confident individuals will attack predators by rearing and then kneeling on them, attempting to crush them. Many llamas and some alpacas will kill foxes this way, if they catch them. (Always remember, however, that a determined predator, or a pack of them, has no trouble in bringing a camelid down. Deaths from dog attacks are common in North America, and have been reported in the UK.)

Kushing

This is a submissive action that denotes lack of both cooperation and resistance. It says in effect, 'I don't know what to do now, so it's up to you to do what ever you want.' Kushing indicates acceptance by a female of mating, and by a male of being mounted by a dominant male. Kushed animals should be treated with caution by handlers, though, because they can very suddenly change their minds and decide to jump up and escape, scattering unwary handlers to left and right! They can also roll onto their sides and lash out with their hind legs.

The Step-Away Reflex

The 'step-away reflex' is the name given to the universal tendency of llamas and alpacas to shy away from approaching touch. Even animals that know you well, and that trust and like you, are impelled to step away if you reach out to touch them. Alpacas and llamas do not indulge in mutual grooming. That is to say, they never lick, nibble, tickle or rub each other for mutual benefit (e.g. parasite removal) or pleasure. Even newly delivered mothers do not lick their babies. The effect of this is that the

This is normal behaviour – don't be alarmed. (Photo: Peter Watson, South West Alpacas)

touch of another animal or human is always unwelcome, presaging at best dominant behaviour by a member of their species, and at worst an attack by a predator.

Llamas and alpacas cannot help having a step-away reflex. It is not personal; they are just made that way. Their handlers must understand that to tolerate touch and not be alarmed or distressed by it is a learned behaviour, and it has to overcome a very deeply rooted sense of alarm.

Sun- and Dust-Bathing

It can be very alarming to see your precious animals lying stretched out on the grass or rolling on their backs in apparent agony, but both sunbathing like a dead thing and rolling like a demented one are normal behaviour for llamas and alpacas.

The 'Beserk Male' Syndrome, or Imprinted Animals

This term is used to describe the behaviour of (usually) male animals that have lost respect for humans. It is almost always, but not exclusively, the result of overhandling a very young cria, which as a result becomes so accustomed to humans that it becomes imprinted by them – that is, it considers humans to be of the same species as itself. When it grows up, it treats humans in the same way that it would treat other alpacas or llamas, subjecting them to spitting, biting, kicking, barging, rearing, and the whole gamut of behaviour at its disposal to establish status and to get its own way. Most humans are physically smaller than llamas or alpacas, so the 'berserk' or imprinted animal reasonably expects to take precedence over them.

More hot-weather behaviour: camelids will enjoy playing with and in water, but remember that prolonged wetting can damage fleece. (Photo: Karen Oglesby, Meon Valley Alpacas)

Usually the overhandling is the result of the young cria requiring to be bottle fed. The humans caring for it are obliged to interact with it several times a day, and simply cannot resist cuddling such an adorably cute and dependent animal. In doing this they inadvertently break down the natural caution and respect between the species. It is not inevitable that bottle-rearing will cause a cria to imprint. Refraining from handling and petting the cria, and returning it to its herd group immediately after feeding, will prevent imprinting from occurring.

The problem with the Berserk Male Syndrome is that, as primates, humans find petting and cuddling a natural means of reassurance and expression of affection for young. Most humans cannot understand that for a different species, this behaviour is wholly inappropriate, and in this case, very harmful.

Rehabilitating a berserk male is often completely impossible, and it remains a danger to humans. As such, it is often necessary to have such animals destroyed to avoid the risk of their causing serious injury.

HANDLING

All domestic animals benefit from being handled by calm, confident people, who do not make sudden or violent movements or noises. At the same time, you should not creep around your animals, since that will ring predator-behaviour alarm bells with them. Talk to them; it will reassure them and give them an easy way of measuring your mood. If you allow yourself to be tense, anxious, or angry, they will realize it, and it will affect their response to you.

Adequate facilities – such that animals that become confused or alarmed cannot escape or injure themselves – are very important. Yards that are sturdy and tall enough (*see* Chapter 3) and arranged so that

This young llama had never been haltered before the occasion of this photograph. Clearly he has rapidly reached a rapport with his young handler. (They don't all learn this quickly!) (Photo: Chris Eke, UK Llamas)

the animals will naturally walk from one to another are a great help.

Catching

The step-away reflex described earlier in this chapter means that even trained animals have a strong tendency to remain out of reach or attempt to escape if approached. Although it is possible to accustom llamas and alpacas to allow you to approach and catch them in an open paddock, for most you will need to drive or tempt them into a catch pen.

The catch pen needs to be small enough that the animal cannot evade contact by moving around it. Typically this will be about 3m (10ft) square, but could be bigger if the maximum width is not more than 3m. Most humans will be unable to dominate a bigger space sufficiently to discourage an animal from running past them. The pen must also be tall enough that a frightened animal will not attempt to jump out of it. For llamas this height is around 2m (6ft) and for alpacas 1.6m (5ft).

If no catch pen is available, then a sufficient number of people who are connected by a rope or who carry outstretched poles (bamboo canes work well for this) or polythene pipes can herd the animals into a corner of the field and form a temporary catch pen. More confident or frightened animals may challenge this type of barrier, making repeated attempts necessary.

Catching. The animal is approached with arms outstretched while being spoken to quietly, so that it knows what you are about to do. It is in a confined space to help it to overcome its innate need to flee a threat. (Photo: Chris Eke, UK Llamas)

Catching. The right arm is used to encircle the neck and discourage the animal from backing away from the halter.

It is better to gather together all the animals in the group because if one is allowed to evade the rope/poles, then others will be encouraged to attempt escape. Singling out one animal will cause it to panic; it is much better and easier to pen up a group and then catch the desired individual from amongst them.

You should approach the animal to be caught with arms outstretched – to make yourself too wide for it to want to run past you – and speak in a calm steady voice, so that it knows what you are going to do. Resist the temptation to sneak up and grab an animal, because this will greatly alarm it and cause it to be more wary and frightened the next time you are close to it.

As you approach the animal, you are aiming to encircle its neck with your arms, bringing yourself to stand next to its shoulder with one arm around its neck, high up, pulling it close to you. Do not stand directly in front of it because it will back away. Also, if it is inclined to spit, being in front puts you directly in the firing line.

If the animal is trained, then stretch a lead or catch rope between your hands so that you can loop this around its neck. Keep the rope high up the neck, the better to control the head, and the loop small enough that the animal cannot withdraw its head. The halter can then be put on.

Control and Restraint

For most purposes the use of a halter is the most convenient method of controlling a llama or alpaca.

Putting On a Halter

Llamas and alpacas take no natural pleasure in having their heads handled. Their normal reaction is to jerk their heads away from contact, and they must be carefully and gently desensitized so that they accept this contact without fear or protest.

I like to halter the animal while retaining hold of the catch/lead rope, high up on the neck. That way, if the animal should be startled and jerk away during the process, I still have control of it. For llamas, I need to put the halter on while standing on the animal's left because they are too tall for me to reach across them to secure the buckle (the halter buckle is always on the left side). Alpacas I can manage from either side.

First adjust the halter to your best guess of the correct size for the animal before you. Standing next to the animal, facing forwards (i.e. the same direction as the animal), open the halter and hold one cheekpiece in each hand. The left hand therefore has both a cheekpiece and the catch rope in it, and the right arm passes behind the animal's head/upper neck.

Then, reach right forward, with the back of the animal's head nesting towards your right shoulder, and hold the open halter out in front of the muzzle so that the animal can see it and will realize what you are going to do. If it is inclined to back away from the halter, your shoulder will steady its head, and also maintain the distance between the halter and its head.

Gently place the noseband over the muzzle, shifting it high up the nose, to fit snugly just below the eyes (*see* photograph opposite). This is very important. If you fail to place the halter high enough up the face, the animal will fear having its nostrils closed by it, and panic. The noseband must have been adjusted so that it is large enough to slide all the way up the nose.

Once the nose is in the noseband of the halter, the animal will often push forward, and you can use this movement to slide your grip up the halter so that you are now holding it by the poll-strap and the buckle. Keeping a moderate pressure on the halter, so that the animal feels physically steadied by it, slip the strap into the buckle and secure it. Tuck in the strap, so that it doesn't flap about. If you need to make any adjustments to other straps to improve the fit of the halter, do that now, while keeping the catch rope around the upper neck.

Removing a Halter

Loop the far end of the lead rope (i.e. the end furthest from the animal's head) around the

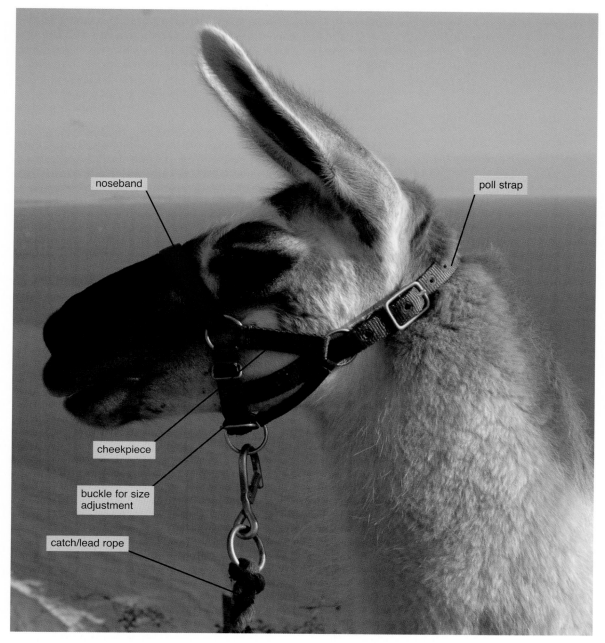

noseband

poll strap

cheekpiece

buckle for size
adjustment

catch/lead rope

A correctly fitting halter. Note how high up the nose and near to the eye the noseband is. (Photo: Chris Eke, UK Llamas)

upper neck, so that you can hold a controlling loop in place.

Hold the lead rope in your right hand and guide the animal close to you so that you will be able to reach behind its head with your right arm and shoulder when the time comes.

Unfasten the buckle with your right hand, transferring the buckle, strap and rope to the

85

Correctly restrained alpaca.

left as they separate, while maintaining a controlling pressure on the lead-rope loop. Maintaining the contact in this way reminds the animal that you are still in charge.

Keep the halter in place with the loosened strap and buckle in your left hand with the lead rope, while you take hold of the halter under the chin with the right hand, reaching around the back of the animal's head. Positively remove the halter from the animal's head (releasing your left hand hold on the strap and buckle, while keeping hold of the lead-rope loop) rather than allowing it to shake off the halter or snatch its head out.

Keep hold of the halter, so that it doesn't drop and startle the animal, and, when the animal is standing quietly, drop the short end of the lead rope and move away from the animal. It is now free.

For a quiet or tall animal, you can hold the rope and straps in the right hand and remove the halter with the left, obviating the need to reach around the back of the head.

Why go to so much trouble when removing the halter? Llamas and alpacas will relish their freedom once released, and look forward to the moment of the halter's removal. Ensuring that you retain control at each step of the unhaltering, means that there will be no opportunity for an impatient animal to take matters into its own hands and escape. They will learn that the best thing to do is to stand quietly until you have finished, and you retain the dominant role by being the one to move away. An animal that plunges and struggles while you are removing the halter is a nuisance, and could even injure your fingers, by jerking them at the wrong moment.

Restraint Without a Halter

For alpacas, this can be achieved with an assistant. The assistant should stand level with the animal's shoulder, facing it. The arm at the head end of the animal should pass under its chin, with the elbow lifted high beneath the chin and the hand on the opposite side of the neck. The other hand should be placed on the withers; light pressure on the withers can be used to discourage struggling.

If the animal does struggle, the arm beneath the chin can be used to push the head rearwards while the hand on the withers can apply pressure to prevent the animal from rearing.

For greatest immobility, push the animal against a wall or fence, but choose one where there is no possibility of its getting a leg stuck through a rail or wire. It is also useful to have some kind of barrier immediately in front of a restrained animal, since its natural direction of flight is forward.

For llamas, restraint by physical means may well require a chute/crush because they can overpower a human (*see* Chapter 3). This fact serves to underline the importance of training llamas to accept handling. In any case, manoeuvring the animal into a secure confined

'Earing.' By firmly grasping the base of both ears the handler has persuaded this animal to stand still for shearing. This technique must not be abused, or the animal will become headshy and not allow its ears to be touched. (Photo: Chris Eke, UK Llamas)

space will often help in persuading it to accept the procedure for which you need to restrain it.

'Earing'

When grasped around the base of the ears, many llamas and alpacas will much more readily accept a mildly unpleasant procedure.

Kush-Tying (Chukkering)

Occasionally it is necessary to cast an animal (bring it to the ground) and tie it to prevent it from struggling. For shearing, this is done with the forelegs and hind legs tied stretched forward and backward. They can also be restrained in the kushed position by passing a rope beneath the hind fetlocks and securing it over the back just in front of the hip bones. This prevents the animal from trying to rise, because it cannot straighten its hind legs. (They rise rear end first, like cattle.) The rope should pass to the inside of the thighs. For complete restraint, a rope can be passed

around each of the bent front legs. Use a thick, soft, cotton rope, so that it does not cut or hurt the animal.

This degree of restraint causes significant distress to the animal, even though it will often seem relaxed, as if it has decided not to fight. Procedures that require this level of restraint should be carried out as quickly as possible, and the animal released to its group as soon as possible. Llamas and alpacas find it deeply distressing to be parted from their group, and handling sessions must be arranged so that groups are maintained for as long as possible, and reconstituted as soon as possible. Prolonged separation from the group can produce a variety of ill-effects. These include immediate nervous and physical collapse – where the animal becomes unresponsive and lethargic, and fails to resume its normal feeding, social behaviour and activity when released – as well as longer term ailments, such as digestive ulceration.

Correctly restrained young llama. A larger animal can not be restrained by a single person. (Photo: Chris Eke, UK Llamas)

Kush-tying or 'chukkering'. This prevents an animal from kicking or running away, but does cause some distress, and the animal should not be left in this position for long periods. In addition to the rope required for kush-tying, a hood or mask will be necessary to prevent spitting.

TRAINING

'You need three things to train an animal: patience, patience and patience. I first came across this advice with regard to dog training, but it applies equally well here. There are several helpful and comprehensive books available on the training and handling of llamas and alpacas. (*See* Further Reading and Bibliography.) My purpose here is to give some general guidelines on techniques that I have found successful, without attempting to cover every possible problem or eventuality. I freely acknowledge that I have incorporated the ideas of Marty McGee, Linda Tellington Jones and John Mallon, and I recommend their books and videos to my readers.

Objectives

When you train your animal, you are trying to persuade it to give up some of its natural behaviour patterns and responses, and to tolerate events and experiences that it finds inherently frightening or threatening. Your gain from this arrangement is a safer, happier, easier interaction with your animals, and theirs is much the same with you: the element of fear and mistrust is removed on both sides.

For training to be successful, it must result in the animals' trusting you, and you them. They must feel reassured and safe in your presence, not threatened and alarmed. Your training programme should bear this in mind at all times.

Training Sessions

Keep these short. The animal can only absorb so much at once. If it reaches a state of dejection and distress, learning cannot occur, and you have broken your faith with the animal. It's supposed to trust you, remember? This technique has been called 'chunking': you break a complex task down into small pieces of manageable size, then deal with them one at a time. John Mallon says, 'Don't be greedy,' meaning that once you have made a significant step of progress, stop – don't try to do everything at one session.

End on a positive note. There is no point in trying to stick rigidly to particular objectives. A small amount of positive progress is much more valuable than a protracted struggle that ends in incomprehension on both sides: the animal wonders what you are trying to do to it, and you wonder why it won't do what you want.

Treat each animal as an individual. You cannot assume that any one animal will respond in the same way as most do. Watch the demeanour, ear position, level of anxiety for each animal, and tailor your training not to overwhelm it at any one session. It will get there in the end; we can't all be Einsteins.

Halter Training

Learning to tolerate restraint from and to obey instructions from a halter is the cornerstone of llama and alpaca training in the UK. The situation is different in South America, but having to share their world with roads and traffic means that here, it's fairly well essential.

Being restrained by the head is not something that llamas and alpacas are naturally inclined to. They have to learn (a) that the halter cannot be escaped, and (b) it will not hurt them. There is a number of different methods for halter training, and in recommending this one to you I do not imply that there is anything wrong with others, just that this one works for me. I learned it from a video produced by John Mallon.

You will need:

- A catch/training pen.
  Trying to train animals that have first to be run down in an open pasture is unnecessarily difficult, if not impossible. Preferably the pen will have solid sides that would not allow an animal's leg to become trapped in them.

- Companion animals.
  If possible, train them in pairs or more (up to six or so). Being separated from their mates will create such a feeling of anxiety

that you will have great difficulty in getting their attention on anything else. At least have other animals visible in a next door pen, unable to wander away and leave the student animal alone. It can be very helpful to have a trained animal present who can have a refresher course and demonstrate how easy it all is to your student animal.

- Halters.
  These absolutely must be adjustable to the correct fit. Permanent damage will be done to the animals' trust in you if they are terrified by an ill-fitting halter, and they may well struggle so violently that they hurt either themselves or you. Your equipment should be in good repair so that it will not break in use.

- Lead ropes.
  Thick, soft cotton ones are the best; thin ones may cut or break under tension. Do not use old rotting lead ropes; if one breaks, valuable learning time is wasted.

- Stout poles or rails to which the animals can be tied.

- Bicycle inner tubes, one per animal.
  They do not need to be brand new, but they must not be weakened or perished in any way. The compliant rubber of the tube is a key element of this technique.

Lesson One

Gather your student animals in the catch pen. Attach a bicycle inner tube around the stout post or railing at each training station, leaving a loop through which you will be able to pass the lead rope. The training stations should be far enough apart that the student animals cannot reach each other. The fencing should not be such that animals can get their legs or feet trapped through it.

Catch the first animal, and put on the halter as described on page 84. (It bears repeating that it is essential that the halter fits).

Speak in a calm encouraging, confident tone throughout, and keep your own demeanour relaxed. (Remember to breathe!)

Shove and cajole the haltered animal to a training station and tie the lead rope to the bicycle inner tube, so that the tube forms the link between the animal and the solid object. Use a quick release knot for the attachment, but arrange the end so that there is no danger of a plunging animal accidentally releasing itself. The total length from the post to the animal's halter should not be more than 1–1.5m (3–4ft).

Move away from the animal, but remain at the scene. Never ever leave a tied animal unattended.

The animal will now probably tug and plunge about, trying to escape the restraint of the halter. It will learn that its struggles produce an unwelcome pressure on the poll. Many animals will quickly learn that they cannot escape, and that it is most comfortable to stand with a slack lead rope until released.

The cushioning effect of the bicycle inner tubes prevents the animal from injuring itself on the halter, and also produces a 'The harder you pull, the harder I pull' response to its movements.

Occasionally an animal will come to rest leaning on the rope and bicycle tube with a taut line, which leaves residual pressure on the poll. For these animals, you need to give them a shove so that the lead rope slackens, releasing the pressure on the head. This gives them a bit of additional help in figuring out how to get comfortable. Keep up an encouraging, calm commentary.

Once your student is standing quietly with the rope slack, approach, untie the halter, and release the animal as described on page 84. If – after a maximum of fifteen or twenty minutes (be guided by your impression of whether the animal is still thinking or 'given up') – the animal has not figured out what to do, shove it forward to slacken the rope, and release it anyway. The penny may well drop tomorrow. Don't be impatient, and don't be greedy.

Halter training. Ryan, frustrated in his attempts to escape, is sulking and has kushed, not knowing what to do next. Note that the lead rope is tight. Now he needs to be shoved forwards to relieve the tension on his head, and to give him a clue about how to do that for himself.

Ryan raises his tail in submission when approached, but has already provided himself with some slack in the lead rope, which he does not pull at in an attempt to escape.

Ryan is now quite relaxed, and has learned to keep his rope slack even when approached.

Ryan is standing quietly and confidently, taking an interest in his surroundings, while accepting the authority and restraint of the halter.

Note that Ryan has other animals close by so that he doesn't become too anxious to pay attention to his lessons.

Group halter-training trips help the animals learn by exploiting their natural tendency to move as a group, in which they feel more confident. (Photo: Chris Eke, UK Llamas)

If your students are used to food treats, a bit of carrot or apple stick given after the lesson can help leave a positive idea in their minds (I do not use concentrate feed for this because it is not a good idea for them to be overfed with concentrates.)

It is normally possible to train up to six animals simultaneously because all you need to do is untangle any particularly violent objectors and shove the 'sulkers' (the ones that just lean back on the line and fail to discover the comfortable position for themselves) forward to give them the idea. Having said that, they are all individuals, and you

must learn to make the judgement of how many animals you can adequately supervise, considering the particular ones in the group.

Use common sense. In my experience animals do not injure themselves or become unduly distressed by this procedure. Tripping, rolling over, or losing balance are rarely enough to cause injury. If your student animals seem alarmingly distressed, either work out why and fix the problem, or seek experienced help. The best age to halter train is at weaning, because the animal is physically smaller to handle, and in a psychological state

1. This young llama's confidence in his young handler fails when he approaches an unfamiliar situation. (Photo: Chris Eke, of UK Llamas)

to accept authority. If you wish to train an older, larger animal, you must accept a greater risk of injury either to it or to you. That does not mean that it's impossible, but the risks are greater, and the task more demanding. I've never had the courage to risk training a pregnant female, for example, although I've seen them throw themselves about for other reasons without ill-effect.

There is no method of training where things will never go wrong. Use your judgement, observe your animals, and be flexible. If you lack the confidence in your judgement to keep the situation reasonably safe and humane, delegate the task to a more proficient stockman, and watch him or her work.

Lesson Two
Begin by repeating lesson one. Once your student animals immediately stand quietly on a slack rope when tied up, you can move on to the next step.

Approach the animal. It will naturally step away. Take hold of the lead rope and, using its learned aversion to pressure on the poll, persuade it to tolerate your approach. Proceed at the animal's pace, and try to do only as much as you can without alarming it into struggling.

You are aiming to get the animal to tolerate your approach, moving around it while very close. It is better to be touch-close because, if an animal kicks, your body will baffle the blow and it will not hurt you as much as it would if you are a few feet away, when the kick will have gathered the momentum to connect much more powerfully. Also, kicking is commonly employed to warn off approach and, if you are already very close, it becomes a less natural behaviour. With very shy animals, you may need to begin the desensitizing with a wand, to give them an extra metre (yard) of 'safe space' while they get used to having you close.

2. *The animal is encouraged by seeing his friends cross the hazard safely. (Photo: Chris Eke, UK Llamas)*

3. *Now worried that he will be left behind, the youngster rushes over the bridge. He has learned that it is safe to cross; now he must learn that it is safe to cross it more slowly.*

If your student animal seems relaxed and calm, start to handle it around the neck and withers, gradually working your way around the body.

Be very patient, and once you have been working in this way for a few minutes, release the animal at a point after calmness and acceptance have been demonstrated.

Lesson Three
Begin by repeating lessons one and two. There is no point in trying to move on until your animal is confident with everything so far.

When your animal is resigned and unafraid to have you move around close to it, and handle its body, head and neck (I tend to leave feet and legs until later, since they are a very worrying area for llamas and alpacas.) then untie the lead rope from the bicycle inner tube.

Your objective is now to persuade the animal to follow the direction of the halter, keeping a slack lead rope. The slackness of the rope is its reward for accepting the authority of the halter. Apply a little pressure on the lead rope. It is usually easiest to get the animal to step to the side at first because a gentle pressure from the side causes it to take a step to rebalance itself. As soon as it takes the step (in fact, as soon as you can see from its weight shift that it is going to step)

Acceptance of Authority

Llamas and alpacas naturally live in hierarchical groups. Accepting the authority of the dominant individual comes naturally to them. In your training, you are assuming the position of the dominant animal. You must behave with the camelid dignity a dominant animal should assume if you want to convince your animals that you are powerful enough to be worth obeying and trusting. This means expecting them to respect your personal space when you move amongst them in the field, and not allowing them to sniff your face or barge you about. They really, really, don't want or need you to cuddle them, trust me.

---

release the pressure on the head. Give a command, like 'Walk on'. It doesn't matter what command you use, as long as you always use the same one. By now the animal should be used to hearing 'Good boy/girl' in a soothing congratulating tone when it gets something right, and you can use this to encourage further steps.

Usually, the student animal will take only a step at a time, and may well take a further lesson or two before it realizes that it can walk normally while being led on a halter. Again, don't be greedy. A step or two is OK. If no further progress is forthcoming, persuade another step out of the animal, and then release it to its reward.

I recommend daily or every other daily sessions for about five or six occasions. For almost all animals this will produce basic biddability on the halter. After that, what you go on to teach will depend on what you need your animals to do. Loading onto a trailer is very useful; following you through or over obstacles is essential for packing llamas. The more you work with your animals, the more confidence they should develop in you. You are aiming for them to get the idea that they can trust you, and if you ask them to do something everything will be OK if they do it.

Handling Feet and Legs
Llamas and alpacas are naturally very sensitive about having their feet and legs touched. If you watch youngsters or adult males playing or fighting in earnest, you will see that biting the front legs is one of the strategies to get an opponent down. Therefore having a limb grabbed by a human is alarming to them, and they will usually want to shy away, or, if it is a back limb, possibly kick.

To handle the legs and lift the feet, you must first desensitize the animal to your touch. By that I mean allow it to grow accustomed to the idea that being touched on the legs does not have to ring alarm bells, that it is safe to let you do it.

It is unreasonable to expect all animals to accept this procedure at the same rate. Those that are more alarmed must be given more time. If you lose patience and grab the foot, holding onto it while the animal struggles, it will quite possibly kush, roll over, kick and plunge, and even if you 'win' by retaining the foot, the next time you move to pick it up, the animal will remember that now it's time to wrestle and fight. I have to confess to having lost patience myself on occasions ('I really need to get these toenails trimmed now') and done just what I have counselled against. No lasting harm has resulted, but the next time I handled the feet I got the expected resistance, and I really had only myself to blame for having to start all over again with getting the animal to agree to cooperate.

The two basic methods I use are 'creeping', or 'wand'.

Creeping

Having trained my animal to allow me to stand close to it and to handle its body, head and neck, I start to work towards the elbow and front of the front limb. As soon as the animal tenses as if to move, I stop moving, and leave my hand, still in firm contact, where it is until the animal relaxes again. If the animal actually moves away I start again, stopping just before the point where it felt it had to move.

Usually, if you speak calmly and encouragingly, and persist a few times, the animal will learn that no harm comes to it if it stands and allows you to hold your hand lightly around the limb, even all the way to the bottom. The same process is used for the hind limb.

Some animals will manage this in one session, some will take several. Don't continue for more than a few minutes, and always stop at a point where the animal is happy to stand relaxed for you.

The final step is to lift the foot from the ground, by leaning your weight through your hips against the animal, to shift its weight away from the foot you wish it to lift, while firmly but gently raising the foot. If this seems to make the animal panic a bit, let it have its foot back while it sorts out its bal-

---

Uncooperative Animals

Where there is an urgent need to handle the feet of an uncooperative animal, you will have either to use a tranquilizer, administered by a vet, or kush-tie the animal. Once in the kushed position, it is possible to reach under the animal, grasp the foot, and wriggle it to a position just to the side of its body, where it may be accessed. Llamas are less inclined to kush, and can often have their feet raised on a rope in a chute/crush if one is available.

---

ance, and try again. Don't keep the foot in the air if it doesn't seem to be able to figure out how to stand on the other three. Repeat until the animal will let you raise a foot without concern.

Wand

I use this method for touchy animals that kick with little excuse. Take a soft-ended nylon wand or a bamboo cane about 1–1.5m (3–4ft) long, and use it, instead of your hand, to start creeping down the limb.

Aim to stop, leaving the wand resting gently against the limb, before the animal feels impelled to move or kick. The technique is exactly the same as for the Creeping method except that the more flighty individuals don't get the same opportunity to kick you.

Once you have desensitized the animal to having its limbs touched, you can substitute your hand for the cane and, using the Creeping technique, get your hand into position for lifting the feet.

Physical Examination

In addition to learning to accept handling of the feet and legs, it is important for animals to become accustomed to inspection of the head, fleece, tail and groin.

Head

Training for this should include teaching the animal to accept inspection of the mouth, eyes, and ears.

Llama being groomed using a long-tined cushioned slicker brush.

It is best for the handler to stand next to the animal and part the lips with the hand that has reached around the back of the head, while another person looks at the teeth. Trying to part the lips while you face the animal places you at risk of being spat at, and causes the animal to back away.

Examination of the Fleece
The animal should stand quietly while the fleece is parted at several sites on the body, neck and legs. Accepting this also facilitates the collection of fleece samples.

Examination under the Tail
Males will have to be accustomed to having the scrotum examined and palpated, and females the vulva. For this it is best to stand to one side of the animal, close to the haunches, and lean across to raise the tail. Move your hand from a 'safe' area gently and slowly to the target area.

Examination of the Groin
This is primarily for females, on whom you may need to place a probe for ultrasound pregnancy examination, or to check the udder. This is a very ticklish area and requires patience.

Grooming
This is normally performed only in llamas, and usually involves raking a coarse, long-tined slicker comb lightly through the upper layers of the fleece to remove debris. Using the flat of your hand in the first instance to accustom the animal to the movement can be

Loading onto a trailer. Load a confident, biddable animal first if you have one.

helpful. It is a very good desensitization exercise in itself, so it should be done early in the animal's training.

Loading onto a Trailer

Almost every animal will need to be taken somewhere by trailer at some time. It is a great blessing if loading and unloading can be accomplished quickly with a minimum of fuss and stress.

1. Make things easy for yourself by having the ramp as flat as possible. On the first few occasions it helps a wary animal to have some straw or familiar bedding on the ramp. If at all possible load a compliant, trained animal first, and secure him in the trailer. Once he sees a friend already safely inside, a student animal will load much more confidently – sometimes a little too confidently!

2. Lead the student animal smoothly into the trailer. Try not to hesitate, but don't rush him – he needs to reassure himself that all is well. If possible, once inside, offer him a

Loading onto a trailer. The presence of an animal already in the trailer is so inviting that even loose animals want to join in the fun.

Loading onto a trailer. Less confident animals will follow the first onto the trailer. (Photo: Chris Eke, UK Llamas)

tasty treat, then unload him first, followed by the experienced animal.

Once the animal has been taught to follow you up a trailer ramp, practise regularly so that procedure does not become rusty. If you are able to leave your trailer open in the field with a haynet inside, so that the animals can practise by themselves, by all means do so. This allows them to become thoroughly familiar with the trailer, and to think of it as a safe place to be.

Unloading

Usually the most difficult thing about unloading is persuading the animal not to rush down the ramp. Some will even attempt to clear the ramp altogether in a mighty leap. This can result in their slipping and falling, or injuring an unwary bystander. The best way to keep control of the situation is to lead the animal down the ramp at a moderate pace, trying to keep its sight line firmly behind you, to discourage it from trying to overtake you.

Short summer treks are ideal for training and conditioning youngsters, but they tire easily, so don't be too ambitious. (Photo: Chris Eke, UK Llamas)

PACKING

There are some excellent American publications on packing with llamas, notably those by Stanlynn Daugherty, Gail Birutta, David Harman and Amy S. Rubin.

Llamas are not fully mature before three years of age and should not carry heavy loads for long distances before then. Even a mature animal that is fully trained should be brought gradually to fitness before being expected to exert himself for sustained periods.

Introducing a pack to a new animal must be a gradual process, like all of the training that has preceded it. If you can acquire a traditional South American woven pannier, it makes the ideal first pack. These are woven from llama fibre and cling naturally to the fibre of the animal's back without the need for a girth strap. This allows the student pack animal to become accustomed to a light load before moving on to packs, which are strapped into position and loaded more heavily. A piece of rough hessian sacking will also suffice, but cannot be loaded as the soft pannier can. The great advantage of these early burdens is that if the animal does become alarmed and plunge, dislodging the pack, it cannot be injured or further alarmed by its falling off.

The llama should be allowed to see and sniff the pack before you expect him to allow you to place it on his back.

A llama string willingly ford a stream after their handler, whom they trust to lead them safely. (Photo: Chris Eke, UK Llamas)

When you stop for a rest, unload your animals and picket them so that they can graze. (Photo: Chris Eke, UK Llamas)

Llamas on the trail will readily browse if given the chance. This particular animal has become too headshy to have a halter put on, but still packs and leads with a neck collar. (Photo: Chris Eke, UK Llamas)

Packing. This is a South American pannier woven from llama fibre. It will remain in place when evenly loaded without the need for a girth. (Photo: Chris Eke, UK Llamas)

Training pannier made from synthetic materials. Like the South American pannier on page 103, it has no girth. (Photo: Chris Eke, UK Llamas)

Full synthetic pack for a day's load. This one has a girth, and it also has breast and breech straps. (Photo: Chris Eke, UK Llamas)

Fastening the girth, or belly strap, on a pack will be the most difficult part for the llama to become accustomed to, and should be accomplished without haste, stopping at any point where the animal starts to become alarmed. Always keep a protecting hand between the buckle and the animal as you fasten it to avoid catching the fleece in the buckle.

CHAPTER 7

Fleece Evaluation

The fleece of llamas and alpacas is correctly referred to as 'fibre' rather than wool The microscopic structure of camelid fibre differs from that of wool, and this affects the way it feels to the touch, and its behaviour during processing. Hair and wool fibres are constructed of a series of scales arranged around a central core. In the case of wool, the scales are 'tiled' with an overlapping pattern; with camelid fibre, the scales are 'paved', with the edges butting up to each other. The fineness of the fibre is related to the thickness of its diameter, which is measured in microns (thousandths of a millimetre). Fibres that are less than 30 microns in diameter are generally too fine to be felt by human skin, whereas those that are greater than this give rise to a 'prickle' sensation.

USES OF FIBRE

In South America, a very large variety of products is made from camelid fibre. These range from rope and harness, through furnishings, to garments of every type. The coarser guard hair of llamas in particular is very tough and durable for the heavier duty items. In the UK, however, there is little demand for llama fibre products, since synthetic alternatives are available fairly cheaply, and the manufacture of the llama fibre versions is labour intensive.

Schematic representation of the difference between sheep wool and camelid fibre. The flatter profile of the camelid fibre explains its silkier touch and its resistance to felting. However, it also means that processing it into a yarn that will not shed is more of a challenge.

sheep wool

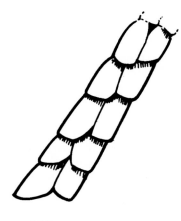

camelid fibre

The outstanding thermal qualities of camelid fibre are illustrated here: there is frost on the outside of these animals' fleeces and yet they remain quite comfortable. (Photo: Chris Eke, UK Llamas)

LLAMA FIBRE

The grooming of llamas often yields a high proportion of the softer undercoat, and from some individual animals this fibre can be of high quality. Many owners have it hand spun into garments for their own use, but grooming does not yield fibre in sufficient quantities to make it commercially viable.

In the UK, shearing of llamas is mainly performed as a husbandry aid. Some animals will grow such a large heavy coat that they rapidly overheat in work, and need to be shorn for comfort. The llama fleece will usually contain a large amount of coarse guard hair, which must be removed before commercial spinning is possible. This is because the thick, straight guard-hair fibres will not process through the same machinery as the finer, crinkled, softer undercoat. Even if the mixed fibre is hand spun, the garments produced from it will retain the coarse, scratchy prickly quality of the guard hair. They should, however, be tough and resistant to wear if spun sufficiently tightly.

ALPACA FIBRE

Since the dawn of their domestication, alpacas have been selected primarily for the qualities of their fleece, and the production of processible fleece is their agricultural purpose. Accordingly, they should, and generally do, have more even, dense, sheep-like fleeces than llamas; alpaca fleece therefore yields a greater proportion of fine fibre uncontaminated by guard hair. Having said this, it is possible to find huge variation in fleece quality in the British alpaca herd, and there is a significant proportion, especially of earlier-imported animals and their descendants that have fairly coarse fibre.

Alpaca fibre is shorn, usually annually, for processing into garment-quality yarn. It can be utilized for either wool or worsted style yarn, suitable for knitwear or tailored garments, respectively. Some of the second-quality fleece may be processed into rugs.

ASSESSMENT OF ALPACA FIBRE

This is quite a specialist skill, and you will need a number of practical lessons in it before you can be confident in your own judgement. There is no substitute for looking at dozens, or better, hundreds, of fleeces, to practise identifying the differences.

The primary difference in fibres lies in its diameter. The diameter of fibre can be measured microscopically. Finer fibres are softer to touch, lighter and less hardwearing. Coarser ones are more durable, but will cause prickliness and scratchiness in a garment. (Can you imagine wanting to wear tweed next to your skin?) The trick is to obtain a good idea of the diameter of the fibres without having with you a precision instrument with which to measure it. Luckily, it is possible to know the precise measurements when samples are sent to laboratories set up for the purpose, so we can discover the truth about any one fleece in time, but when making buying decisions, you often need to have some idea without waiting to have samples analysed. There is also the theoretical possibility that the sample the lab got did not come from the animal you are looking at, so you need to

A llama shorn to help him keep cool in the summer. (Photo: Dick Hobbs)

A fleece evaluation class. Attendance at such tutorials is essential if you wish to become competent at fleece evaluation. (Photo: John Gaye, Alpacas of Wessex)

A champion huacaya fleece. (Photo: John Gaye, Alpacas of Wessex)

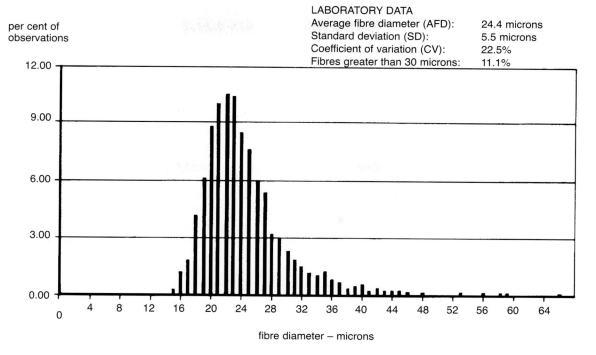

LABORATORY DATA

Average fibre diameter (AFD):	24.4 microns
Standard deviation (SD):	5.5 microns
Coefficient of variation (CV):	22.5%
Fibres greater than 30 microns:	11.1%

This is what you get back from the lab after your fleece samples have been analysed. Included in the report will be the animal's name, breed, sex, colour, ID, and age. The location of the sample (the part of the body from which the fleece was taken) will also be indicated. Refer to the notes on interpretation of histograms (see below), and don't give up – you will soon get the hang of it. (Reproduced with the kind permission of Yocom-McColl Testing Laboratories, Inc., Denver, USA)

be able to tell a good fleece from a bad one from its look and feel.

Fleece Samples

These are normally taken from the middle of the blanket area, about halfway along the animal and a couple of handspans down from the spine. This area usually most reliably yields the best fleece on analysis. An area of roughly 8cm (3in) square is shorn close to the skin, and the handful of fleece handled carefully to keep all the fibres together and facing the same way. Often samples are taken at shearing, but they may be taken at any time once the fleece is more than about 5cm (2in) long. Bare areas of skin will result in loss of marks in the show ring if discovered by the judge, so samples should be taken with this

risk in mind, or perhaps delayed until after the show.

Bear in mind that the sample represents the best fleece the animal has to offer (although research has demonstrated that finer micron counts can be found on parts of the neck).

Histograms

The fleece sample is analysed in the lab, where the diameter of a many fibres is measured and expressed in microns (one millionth of a metre, or one thousandth of a millimetre). The results are usually presented as a graph, called a histogram (*see* above).

Because each fibre will be slightly different from all the others, it is usual to talk and think about the average (or mean) fibre diameter. Generally speaking, the finer the better. Fibres over 30 microns in diameter can be felt by human skin as prickly, so such fleece will not be suitable for use in next-to-skin garments. However, fibres under 10–12 microns in diameter are very delicate, and will not wear well. The selling point of all luxury fibre is its ability to retain strength at low diameters that feel soft to the skin.

1. Look at the overall shape of the histogram. The best fleeces produce a tall, thin, straight sided curve, with minimal 'tails' at each side. This shape means that many fibres in the sample were of the same diameter. This is desirable because it translates into more reliable behaviour during processing, and a more even look to the yarn and fabric. A flat, low, hill of a curve implies the opposite – that the fleece sample contained fibres of widely differing diameters, i.e. lacking in uniformity, and would therefore not be expected to process as well. A guide to the AFD is given by how close to the left-hand side of the graph the peak of the curve appears.

2. Look at the average fibre diameter (AFD) figure.
   The AFD or MFD (mean fibre diameter) is calculated by adding together the diameter of each fibre in the sample, and dividing by the number in the sample. It gives some information, but because having lots of very fine fibres to balance out lots of very coarse ones can still yield a relatively low AFD, it tells you nothing about the uniformity and processing quality of the fleece. In general, though, the lower the AFD, the better.

3. Look at the standard deviation (SD) figure.
   The standard deviation measures the fatness of the curve, by telling you how far from the mean figure the sides of the curve are at a point that incorporates a standard proportion of the fibres in the sample. This is an important guide to the uniformity of the thickness of the fibres, and the lower the better.

4. Look at the coefficient of variation figure (CV)
   This expresses the standard deviation as a proportion of the AFD. (Don't glaze over at this point: if you read this at least three times, you will start to understand how it works, and it can give you valuable information, without which you will be at a serious disadvantage in assessing the value of an animal.) The CV tells you how important the SD is in the grand scheme of things, so it's another measure of uniformity, but relates it to the average thickness of the fibres. Again, the CV should be as low as possible, and some theorize that if the CV is lower than the AFD, then the animal is less likely to 'blow out' with age. I have no data that prove or disprove this.

5. Look at the percentage over 30 microns.
   This tells you what percentage of the fibres is over 30 microns thick. Of course, it is another measure of uniformity, or lack of it, but the magic 30 micron figure is the thickness at which a fibre will cause 'prickle' on human skin. Once more, the lower this figure is, the better. For a fleece of AFD around 20 micron, a quality animal should have no more than 1 per cent fibres over 30 microns.

6 Look at the time of sampling.
   Minor variations in fibre diameter are caused by variations in levels of nutrition. In the UK, fibres that are harvested in the spring will be thinner than those harvested late in the summer. Also, compare the date of the sample with the date at which you are assessing the animal. Is this a current sample? Or an historical one, which will flatter the animal? Was it baby fleece? This will always be the finest fleece the animal ever produces.

Alpacas have Guard Hair, Too

If you look at an alpaca in fleece, you will be able to see that around the chest, belly and legs, there is a silky, hairy look to the coat.

These parts of the fleece have abundant guard hair and must be separated from the premium 'blanket' during shearing. Guard hair in the blanket area translates into 'Fibres Over 30 Microns' in the fleece sample. Areas of fleece that are heavily populated by guard hair are destined for processing into coarse fabrics and rugs.

Since the presence of guard hair limits the amount of premium fleece that an individual animal can produce, those that have a minimum of it, and have it restricted to a smaller area of the body, are the ones that are desirable for breeding purposes. Where the guard hair has been trimmed from the animal, for showing, only the assessment of a tiny hank of plucked fleece (ask permission!) will reveal it.

BLOWING OUT

This term is used to describe the tendency of fleeces to become coarser as the animal gets older. In some animals the effect is quite dramatic, and can cause the fleeces from animals older than about three years to be more or less commercially worthless. In all animals it is expected that the first fleece will be the finest, but the ability to retain most of the fineness into maturity is enormously valuable and, crucially, inherited.

ASSESSMENT OF HUACAYA ALPACA FLEECE

This should be done before the animal has been shorn. (Refer also to Chapter 9 for fleece assessment checklist.) A shorn fleece can be assessed, but you have to be (a) sure that it is from the right animal and (b) sure that you will be able to look at it sufficiently thoroughly to assess the distribution of premium versus second-grade fibre. (It is absolutely essential if assessing a shorn fleece to know its weight, with and without 'seconds'.)

It is always much easier to assess a fleece while it is on the animal. Always get permission from the owner to assess the fleece. The

---

Characteristics of Alpaca Fleece

- *Fineness* refers to the AFD, or micron count.
- *Softness* is subjective, and simply refers to that quality when the fleece is grasped and squeezed.
- *Crimp* refers to the small corrugations visible in most fleeces. Ideally these should all lie together, giving the parted fleece a uniformly wavy look. (Although there is no evidence that uniformity of alignment of crimp enhances the processing characteristics of fibre, it looks nice.)
- *Lustre*, or brightness, is the term used to indicate the ability of the parted fleece to reflect light.
- *Density* describes how closely packed the fibres are in the skin, and therefore has a positive relationship with the weight of fleece a particular animal will cut.
- *Uniformity of colour* means that the overall colour of the animal is constant from fibre to fibre, and across the body surface. Some animals have a mixture of depths of colour in their fleeces, and or different coloured fibres adjacent to each other, or patches of different coloured fleece.
- *Character/Handle* is another subjective term, which tries to give an indication of a positive sense of quality. It may be the best that human senses can do in assessing uniformity of fibre diameter.

---

disruption caused by your examination could cause problems in the show ring, for which you will not wish to be responsible.

The characteristics used in the assessment of the value of the fleece are: fineness, softness, crimp, lustre, density, uniformity of colour, and character, or handle. (*See* box above for definitions of these characteristics.)

1. Look at the animal from a distance.
   Does it look compact, with no partings appearing on the topline? This is an indication of density, which will produce a heavier fleece.

   Does it have a fine misty outline over its main surface? This is a sign of guard hair throughout the fleece, because it grows straighter and longer than the undercoat,

Stand back and look at the overall outline. (Photo: John Gaye, Alpacas of Wessex)

and appears as a fine fringe above the general level of the fleece.

Does the animal have a dense, rounded bonnet? This often indicates overall density in the fleece. How far down the legs does the springy, woolly looking fibre go? This quality is referred to as coverage. Heavy, hairy leg fibre is not valuable, but visibly woolly looking fibre may be if the level of guard hair is low.

2. Push your loosely clawed hand into the fleece at a number of points.
   Does it spring back at you, pushing your hand out of it slightly? This is another indication of density. Your hand needs to be dry and warm to have sufficient sensitivity for this task.

3. Look closely.
   If you need to wear reading glasses, put them on now. (Apart from anything else, it will make you look as if you know what you are doing!) Part the fleece (*see* photograph opposite). You need to be in a good light, and the fleece really needs to be dry, because your fingers lose sensitivity if they are wet.

   The fleece should part cleanly with minimal tangling or matting, which is called cross-fibring.

   How wide is the line of skin you can see at the parting of the fleece? The narrower the better, because that indicates densely packed fibre follicles in the skin. Does the fibre part into square-edged blocks (bundles)? This property also indicates density and is termed staple definition.

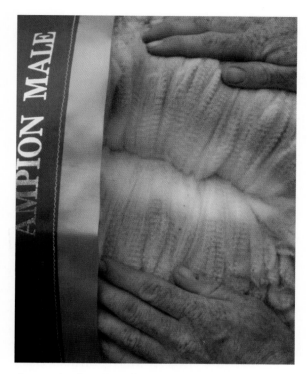

A superior huacaya fleece. Refer to section on fibre assessment to see how it measures up. (Photo: John Gaye, Alpacas of Wessex)

Are all the fibres in the parting the same colour, or is there a mixture of different coloured ones? Uniformity of colour is desirable.

How uniform and fine is the crimp? Marks for style will be awarded for uniformity and tightness of the crimp wave, although there doesn't seem to be an absolute relationship between tightness of crimp and fineness of fleece; some fine fleeces have quite a bold crimp.

If you push your flattened hands gently together as they lie on the fleece, to make the fleece arch upwards slightly, how does the light reflect from it? Part of the value of alpaca fabric comes from its ability to return the light in a slight sheen. White fleeces should exhibit a sun-on-snow type of brilliance, and other colours should show a sheen reminiscent of a molten surface.

4. Repeat the fleece parting.
   Do this at different sites on the animal's body, neck and topknot. The more uniform the findings at each site, the better. Check how far down the belly and legs the best-quality fleece goes, and where it gives way to hairier, coarser fibre.

5. Pull out a few fibres.
   Have permission from the owner to do this: if allowed, do it by gripping a few fibres with thumb and one fingernail. For white fleece, lay them over a dark sleeve (for other colours use a contrasting background) and look at how fine they are, and whether there are any that are thicker and straighter looking. These odd thicker fibres indicate medullation, the presence of an air chamber down the centre of the fibre. They are undesirable because, being thicker, they reduce the softness of the fleece and, if thick enough, contribute to prickle in the fabric.

6. Roll the tiny bundle you have plucked between finger and thumb.
   There should be minimal sensation of anything at all being there – the less the better. Finally, take hold of both ends of the hank and give it a good tug. This is to test for weakness in the fibre, known as 'tenderness'. (Sounds nice, but not a good thing.)

7. Ask the weight of the yield at the last shearing.
   Also ask for how much growth (i.e. was it twelve months' worth of fleece, or more, or less?) and whether there are any current and historical fibre data from a lab sample. (Remember that the dates of collection of the samples are critically important because of the possibility of an animal's 'blowing out'.) If there are, see how well it accords with what you would have predicted, and see if there is a change over time. Fleeces that 'blow out' with age will demonstrate this property clearly with sequential lab samples, so having up-to-date results

is important. Obviously, you have only a person's word that the fibre sample was taken when they say it was: if they keep it for two years and then send it to the lab, it will give a false impression of the quality of the fleece because, in all but the most exceptional animals, the fibre growing now will not be like the fibre harvested two years ago. If you are spending a lot of money, consider asking to harvest and send your own fibre sample, on the understanding that if the results are as predicted you will definitely buy him.

ASSESSMENT OF SURI ALPACA FLEECE

Once again, have permission from the owner for any of the 'hands-on' part of this assessment. Bear in mind that once shorn, suri animals take two to three years to develop their lock styles again. For this reason suri fleece is often left on longer than the standard year

for huacayas. However, if left on too long, the fleece will become matted, as it will for huacayas. Once this happens it is pretty well commercially useless.

1. Stand back and look at the animal.
   The fibre should hang in long, clearly defined ringlets, called locks. These should not be matted and tangled, or soft ('lofty') looking. More tightly curled locks usually indicate a greater fleece weight.

2. Watch the animal move in good light.
   An impression of the lustre of suri fleece is really only possible when the animal is moving. The light should seem to spill off the rippling fleece like water.

3. Inspect the locks closely.
   (Reading glasses again.) Are the locks distinct, neat and clean looking? They should be well separated from each other, with a regular rate of twist, which starts as close

The densely corded look of this suri fleece is consistent over the whole body and legs. (Photo: John Gaye, Alpacas of Wessex)

Close-up view of the lock formation. (Photo: John Gaye, Alpacas of Wessex)

as possible to the skin. The locks should feel cool to the touch and distinctly silky. The lock style of fleece should cover as much of the animal as possible; usually there are only two grades of fleece on a suri, as opposed to the three different qualities found on huacayas. More lofty, fluffy suri fleece will have a poorer lock definition.

4. Part the locks.
   You are looking for a narrow strip of skin in the parting, again indicating greater density of follicles, and a uniform rate of spiralling in the ringlets. It is not agreed that any particular style of lock is preferable, but a tighter spiral usually indicates a higher fleece weight.

5. Repeat across the fleece.
   Check coverage and uniformity: is the lock style consistent; does it cover the animal?

6. Pluck a tiny hank.
   With the owner's permission, do this as for huacaya fleece and assess for medullation over a sleeve, and fineness as before (*see* Assessment of Huacaya Fleece, Step 5). Finally, take hold of both ends of the hank and give it a good tug to test for weakness (tenderness) in the fibre.

7. Ask the weight of fibre at last shearing.
   Again, also ask for any fibre data that may exist. The interpretation of histograms is basically the same as for huacaya fleece.

Parted suri fleece showing the brilliance of its lustre. (Photo: John Gaye, Alpacas of Wessex)

PRODUCING FLEECE FOR COMMERCIAL USE

Shearing

The process of shearing was dealt with in Chapter 5, but there are several factors that you need to be especially aware of when shearing fleece with the intention of selling it or using it.

Fleece Preparation

If you wish your fleece to have any commercial value, preparation for shearing and shearing itself are critically important. Even hand-processing requires the fibre to be clean and uncontaminated by vegetable matter and, for machine processing, it is even more important, since the machinery will be damaged by contaminated fleece. It is astonishing how many dewy-eyed alpaca owners there are who think that the stinking, tangled, jumbled, grassy, thorny, mucky heap they have lying at the back of the shed must be worth a fortune because 'alpaca is a luxury fibre'. Sadly, no one can do anything with it while it is mixed up with all the other elements of the heap, and sorting it out for processing would be very labour-intensive, certainly wiping out any profit on it.

Before shearing, the animals must be kept in a clean paddock, with no vegetation that has gone to seed. Grass seeds, burrs, dock flowers, brambles and so on, are all very bad things to have in fleece, and picking them out is impractical, because it takes so long. It is also desirable not to have muddy rolling patches in your field, since llamas and alpacas love to roll and will cake themselves with mud or worse (cow muck is especially difficult to remove) if given the opportunity. You may need to choose your shearing time with pasture growth in mind, to avoid long

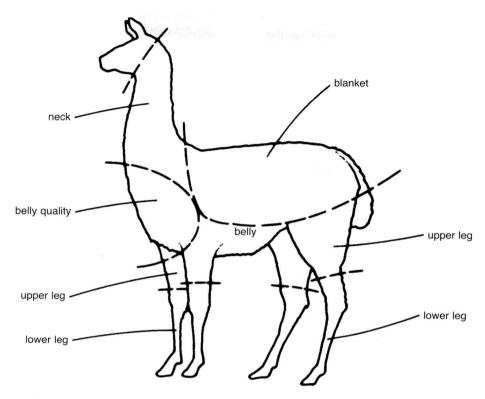

Approximate boundaries of the areas of differing quality of alpaca fleece. These areas should be separated from each other at shearing, so that only similar-quality lots of fibre are presented for processing.

fleeces and grass seeds from coming into contact. Baby fleeces (i.e. the first fleece shorn from an animal up to a year old) are especially good at picking up any kind of contamination; if not shorn at a year of age, the baby tips retain their ability to catch debris until they are shorn. This leads to a first fleece with dirty, ragged-looking tips. Some breeders shear their show animals while they are still baby crias to get a better-looking fleece at the end of the first year.

Shearing Conditions

The conditions in which the animals are shorn are critical. First and foremost, the fleece must be dry. Shearing wet animals is almost impossible, since the shears do not cope well with wet fibre (even a sweating animal can cause the shears to rise up over the

fibre and to fail to cut it cleanly and evenly), and wet fibre will heat and rot very quickly, so you would need facilities to dry it immediately. If the weather is wet or dewy, the animals need to stand under cover overnight to ensure that they are dry when they are shorn.

Cleanliness

The area chosen for shearing should be spacious enough to accommodate the stretched-out animal, the equipment, the shearer and helper, and be capable of being swept absolutely clean between animals. If this cannot be achieved, then the newly shorn fleece will become contaminated and devalued for processing. The flooring should also be capable of being wiped clean, since the occasional animal will urinate during shearing. If your barn has a mud floor, a tarpaulin should be laid over it.

Skirting

This is the process of separating the finest quality fleece from the second and third quality parts. The best time to remove the second quality fleece from the more valuable blanket is at shearing, so make sure that you have enough help for someone to devote themselves to this task. Once the fleece has been bundled together, it is a much more difficult and lengthy job to sort the best from the rest. A good shearer will be prepared for you to, or (depending on what he's charging you) even have his or her helper, remove the skirtings and place them in a separate bag or bin. There are three basic classes on an individual fleece: blanket, seconds (neck and better parts of legs and belly)and 'rubbish' the very hairy parts of chest, legs, belly, and any mucky, smelly, or fleece tangled with seeds, burrs, hay or other vegetable matter.

Weighing

Blanket and seconds skirtings will normally be processed separately from each other, but the advantage of placing them in with, but separated from, the blanket is that you can weigh the whole fleece and record the individual animal's yield. A spring balance will be sufficient to get a good idea of how much fleece each animal produces.

Classing

For processing, individual fleeces must be mixed to produce quantities large enough to occupy the machinery concerned. It is important to keep the fibre in lots of uniformly similar quality and colour, otherwise the settings on the machinery will not be able to cope with fibres of vastly differing thickness, strength and degrees of straightness versus waviness. Mixtures of colour will produce contamination of the colour of the final fabric. If you wish to sell your fibre, it is worth much more to a processor if you have sorted it into lots of different classes. Examples of different classes are:

- Superfine white baby blanket fleece;
- Fine white blanket;
- Coarse white blanket.

Usually these classes correlate with certain average fibre diameters, so it is really useful to have taken fleece samples from your animals so that you have a rough idea where they come in the hierarchy. The superfine baby blanket will usually be up to about 21 microns AFD (your processor will let you know what its particular classes are), the fine will be up to about 25 microns, and the coarse above that. There will be a significant amount of fibre from skirtings and older animals that will be what I call 'rug quality', and suitable only for processing into high-wear, low skin-contact products, such as rugs or carpets.

Training for Classing

I have given the guidelines here for the theory of classing, but there is no substitute for practical training and experience in handling and sorting fleece. Join your local association and go to some training days to be shown how to do it. Some processors have the expertise and manpower to class for you, but they will obviously have to charge you for this service. The less work your fleeces are for them, the less they will charge you for sorting them.

Storing

Paper bags (for example unused potato sacks) are best for storing your fleece prior to its being processed because they allow some escape of water vapour (the fleece will have some natural dampness just from the humid environment of the skin of the animals). Plastic sacks, especially if not perforated, allow condensation to develop, and wetness will degrade the fleece. Woven nylon sacking, which also allows moisture to escape, is also suitable. Whatever material you choose, it must be clean and not able to stain or contaminate the fleece.

CHAPTER 8

Fleece Marketing

by John Gaye
(of Alpacas of Wessex)

THE UNIQUE SELLING POINT

What is so special about alpaca fibre? What qualities does it have that other natural fibres lack? How does it compare with other 'noble fibres' such as cashmere, silk or mohair, and why is it better and more expensive than wool?

Until the late part of the 1990s, in the British market place alpaca fibre was virtually unknown other than to those who had travelled in South America or who had heard about it from their grandparents. It was a fibre that had been considered the finest in the land during Victorian days but since then it had not been widely available in Britain. Suddenly it was regaining its position as a 'noble fibre' and making its mark amongst those who were keen on having really special garments without paying the huge sums that were demanded by the retailers of the best cashmere products.

Alpaca fibre should not be compared as better or worse than cashmere. Both fibres have their virtues, but essentially they have a very different feel or 'handle' to them and of course alpaca fibre comes in two different types – Huacaya and Suri. Huacaya alpaca fibre can be utilized in any product that you might expect to be made from sheep's wool. It can be found in all types of knitwear, in scarves and shawls and in woven form in suiting or material for coats or jackets. You can turn it into covers for seats, fill duvets with it or create wonderful rugs or carpet. It is extremely versatile. The very best fibre can be turned into products that will grace the catwalks of the world's best fashion shows; the lowest quality fibre can still produce luxurious carpeting. Suri fibre is considered to be even better in many ways than huacaya although the complexity in the processing is such that only a few processors have the technical knowledge to do it justice. Suri fibre tends to be kept for material that will go into jackets, coats or skirts.

Alpaca fibre qualities start with its handle. This differs significantly from cashmere, which is highly valued for its glorious softness and comfort against the skin. Good-quality alpaca is soft and can be comfortably worn against the skin, but it has much more of a silky feel and look to it. When you squeeze a pure alpaca garment it almost feels damp to the touch. Its fineness varies according to the age and quality of the animal it came from, but the very best alpaca fibre can be as fine as 15 or 16 microns in diameter. More commonly the highest graded alpaca will be somewhere in the region of 18–22 micron, which will be sufficient to go into the very best garments. This grade of fibre is more commonly known as 'Baby Alpaca' – it need not be taken from young animals but the tendency is for the diameter of the fibre to broaden, or strengthen, as the animal gets older.

119

Alpaca fleece is prized by hand spinners, and direct sales to them can provide a small income at better margins than processing fleece commercially. Note the hand-operated drum carder in the background (top right). (Photo: Chris Eke, UK Llamas)

If you examine the fibre under a microscope alongside a fibre of wool you will see that it lacks the minute little scales of the woollen fibre; this gives it a huge advantage because it is these little scales that can lead to the irritation that people with sensitive skin tend to suffer. However this 'prickle factor' can still be present in alpaca if the fibre has not been properly sorted by the producer or de-haired during the processing. The ideal alpaca will produce fibre with almost no primary fibres, or guard hair. These fibres are easily visible in a fleece because, unlike the desirable secondary fibres, they are straight and without any crimp. Consequently when the fibre is spun into yarn these straight, usually stronger, fibres tend

not to blend in with the others and thus produce fibre ends that can lead to prickle.

ESTABLISHING A COMMERCIAL ALPACA INDUSTRY

Anyone who has visited the vast alpaca textile mills in Peru will have been impressed with the scale of the operation. Huge buildings house a myriad of machines that commercially process the fibre produced from about 3 million alpacas. They operate, as all large processing plants must do, all year round and are constantly turning out various grades of yarn in many different colours – some natural but most dyed according to the demand of the fashion market. At the heart of the operation however are the sorters and graders of the raw fibre that appears in the warehouse in truckloads off the altiplano. These women (and there is never a man to be seen on the sorting floor) spend their day carefully going through the various piles of fleece making their own little piles according to the quality of the fibres presented. In this way the mill can then have a complete run of fibre producing a yarn of consistent quality for specific uses. Their skills are vital to the whole operation and it is a labour-intensive operation that cannot be emulated outside of an economy that has low wages.

Thus for a newly developing national alpaca industry it is a real challenge to be able to jump the very first hurdle, which is the presentation of fleece of a consistent quality and in a quantity that would satisfy a commercial operation using mills on this scale. Mills want tons of fibre, in bales, all of the same quality and of the same colour, not individual fleeces, still in their plastic bags, which have not been properly sorted. So the first challenge must be to get producers to be able to sort and grade their own fleeces with integrity and accuracy. This is complicated by the varying natural colours that are presented. The wide palette of colours may well appeal to a certain market but, when trying to build up a commercial quantity of high-quality fibre, this variation just reduces the amount that is available in one single colour.

Thus it is necessary for new national fibre industries to accept that they will have to start with small quantities of fibre and find small mills specializing in the various noble fibres who are prepared to process and spin relatively small quantities of fleece. To do this however still requires producers to combine together and cooperate in producing sufficient quantity to make the operation worthwhile.

The alternative is to start with the cottage industries that exist in many first world nations and to become involved with the enthusiasts who love working with different fibres to make various garments, usually in natural colours. The danger of this is the production of poor-quality items that do not reflect the potential that is inherent in high-quality alpaca fibre and thus reducing the perception of alpaca in the fashion market.

THE BRITISH MARKET

In the early days of the British alpaca industry a co-operative was put in place to ensure that all producers banded together with a view to bulking up their fibre so that it could more quickly become commercial in both quantity and quality. The aim was to take control of all the various stages of processing, turn the fibre into product and then market the product, thus adding value to the fibre at all stages and retaining control and a much better margin for the principal product from the back of the alpaca.

This co-operative went through various stages, including an initiative that linked into the Australian Co-operative whereby raw fibre was sent out and finished garments were sent in return. This helped the Australians, who were short of quantity, and it gave the British Co-operative an immediate product to turn into cash flow.

However the co-operative suffered various problems and many breeders lost faith in it; so, just as it was on the point of becoming profitable, it ran short of both capital and fibre and as a result went into suspended animation so that it is still sitting there waiting for a successful initiative to take it forward once again sometime in the future.

Meanwhile, at the time of writing, there are many initiatives to turn alpaca fibre into product. This product may just be yarn, or knitting wool, for home knitters to enjoy making into garments of their own choice. However many have taken their fibre, had it processed into yarn and then had it knitted or woven into various products for them to sell into the market.

There are now a number of mills that will spin the fibre in small quantities, but it is very important to know exactly what you wish to

Products manufactured from British alpaca fleece. (Photo: John Gaye, Alpacas of Wessex)

produce at the end of the whole operation. There is no point in expecting items that will be 'luxurious' or worn next to the skin if the quality of the fibre is not sufficiently good. Ideally this sort of item should be made only from the Baby Alpaca end of the scale, i.e., somewhere below 22 microns in diameter.

For the fibre that is in the order of between 22 and 26 microns there is a range of options and this quality could certainly go into knitting yarn for sweaters, socks, scarves or other knitwear. However, even to the average person it will definitely be of a lesser quality to the touch than that of the sub-22 micron.

Spinning is but one part of the whole process of turning fibre into a finished product, and it is important for anyone starting out on an initiative of their own to understand not only the various processes but also something of the language of textile processing.

SKIRTING AND SORTING

Raw fibre taken from the back of the alpaca has to be sorted by the producer to ensure that all the primary fibres are removed and all the detritus, dust, second cuts and other fibres that will contaminate the fibre to be sent for processing are identified and removed. This is best done at the time of the shearing but can be done at any time before the fleece is sent off. It is vital to ensure that there is no contamination that will downgrade your whole fleece. It is a skill that all alpaca owners should acquire – it is not something that you can expect the shearer to do for you.

It is at the sorting stage that the quality of the fleece is assessed (this should also be done objectively by taking a sample from the mid-side at shearing, and having it analysed by a laboratory for its qualities). The producer will need to know how much of each quality there is so that he or she can decide what is to be done with it. The other vital aspect of sorting is to get the colour right. If it is white it must all be white; if it is fawn or brown the shades should all be the same. Black fleece should have no white hairs unless you wish to have it dyed.

SCOURING

This is a washing process, carried out as the first stage in the commercial processing, which essentially takes out any of the small items of contamination from the fleece that the producer has missed. It is the cleaning process that stops vegetable matter, or worse, from getting into the final yarn. For hand spinners it is not essential, but for any form of commercial processing it is vital, as bits of straw do not enhance a yarn or a nice alpaca sweater. The scouring process will also wash out any natural greasy oil, urine or sweat from the fibres. Once scoured the fibre is then dried.

CARDING

After scouring, the fleeces are carded, which separates the individual fibres and removes any further contamination that may have survived to this stage.

COMBING

The aim of combing, which is particularly important if using the worsted spinning process, is to straighten the fibres and to separate the short from the long fibres. Without combing, the yarn would fall apart in the finished garment and little noils would appear, which are essentially the short fibres being unable to hold together in the structure of the wool. As a result of carding and combing the fibres are turned into a soft twistless rope called 'tops'.

Skeins of yarn for hand knitters spun from pure British alpaca in natural colours. (Photo: Jean Field, Devon Alpacas)

SPINNING

This is the process whereby tops are turned into yarn. However, there are two types of spinning – worsted and woollen. Woollen spun yarns typically go into yarns for sweaters, tweeds and carpets while the worsted process produces yarn for woven garments. However, there is a certain amount of crossover in the use of worsted yarn as it can also be turned into woollen type garments. The critical difference for the owner of the fibre is that the woollen process is better when there is a variety of lengths of fibre, because the worsted process will reject shorter lengths during carding. This is because, when spun, the shorter lengths will separate and come away as noils. For the textile person, the type of spinning process will depend entirely on what they want as the finished garment.

When the fibre is ready to go into the spinning process it is essential that the decision on the final product has been made. The spinner will want to know what ply of yarn to make, and whether it is to be blended with any other fibres. If using a variety of natural colours, you might wish to create a melange using different colours of single ply in a four-ply yarn. This is a very popular way to create a warm autumnal coloured yarn. Alpaca can be blended with all sorts of different fibres and it may be advantageous to add some wool, silk or cotton to the yarn.

WHERE TO TAKE YOUR FIBRE

At the time of writing, about £90,000 buys you a mini-mill. That is far and away above what most alpaca breeders are prepared to invest in their fibre. However some enthusiasts have invested in mini-mills and have been helped in their endeavours by generous local government grants. Thus alpaca producers have an ever-growing choice of processors available to handle small quantities of fibre. In addition there are larger mills that can handle alpaca fibre and whose owners are keen to support the ever-growing number of producers who want to take an initiative in adding value to their product by processing and manufacturing finished garments.

A list of the mini-mills offering a service to producers can be found in the Useful Addresses section at the end of this book.

CHAPTER 9

Assessment and Showing

When you begin your search for animals to buy, you will discover that there is a large range on offer. If you are not to waste your money on unsuitable stock, you need to know how to assess the qualities of an animal presented to you. Throughout this chapter I have referred to an animal in the singular, but my view is that it is not acceptable on welfare grounds to keep these strongly social and herd-oriented animals without company of their own kind.

Assessing animals is very much a hands-on skill, so you must overcome your diffidence and expect to handle the animal to make your judgements. If you have a knowledge-able friend who already owns animals, it can be a great benefit if you can be allowed to handle them before you go shopping for your own. This will allow you to develop an assessment routine, and also give you invaluable knowledge about what is 'normal'. Failing that, attend a course to get the same experience. They may seem expensive, but you are probably contemplating spending quite a lot of money, and the amount you spend on expanding your knowledge is small in comparison to what it may save you.

Many experienced camelid keepers use a points system to assess animals. The advantage of this is that it gives you a much more unbiased assessment of the overall qualities of each animal when compared with others. This, as Amanda Van den Bosch says, 'Keeps

you honest.' By this she means that if you happen to have a particular preference for large eyes, or a dense topknot, or even long eyelashes, a points system will prevent your weighting that particular characteristic disproportionately, and conssequently overvaluing animals that you are inclined to fall in love with. Giving way to such personal prejudices is unimportant if you have no requirement to make financially sound decisions, but if you expect any return from your enterprise you must school yourself to value the same characteristics as those that the rest of the market values.

BREEDING

Unfortunately, there is no guarantee that a perfect animal standing before you will throw equally perfect offspring, even if it is mated to another perfect-looking individual. Therefore, if you are selecting animals for breeding, the relationship between phenotype and genotype is very important.

Phenotype Versus Genotype
An animal's phenotype is its physical appearance, in other words the genetic characteristics that are visibly expressed and therefore apparent to you when you look at the animal. An animal's genotype is its genetic make-up – the characteristics that it carries genetically, but that are not visibly

This elite male looks as though his front legs are not perfectly straight in this photograph. Even if this should be the case when he is viewed from the front, his fleece and other characteristics would justify using him as a breeding male. Avoid mating him to a female with knock knees, though. (Photo: John Gaye, Alpacas of Wessex)

expressed; these, however, may appear in its offspring. Clearly you want to select the specimen with the best possible physical appearance – one whose phenotype is desirable – but in order to know the extent to which its offspring will resemble it, you need data on offspring already born if it is avail-

able: this will give you an insight into the animal's genotype and ability to stamp these characteristics on its offspring.

Progeny Testing

This is the practice of collecting data on the offspring of breeding animals to check the

This is a fabulous-looking alpaca. Remember to assess the whole animal methodically, so as not to miss any defects dwarfed by his presence and overall appeal. (Photo: John Gaye, Alpacas of Wessex)

degree to which they are passing on particular characteristics to their offspring. For example, if you are interested in the fineness of fleece, you might look at the improvement in micron count over the mothers' counts of a group of cria all sired by the same animal. This gives you an idea of how much effect the sire's genes have had on this characteristic.

127

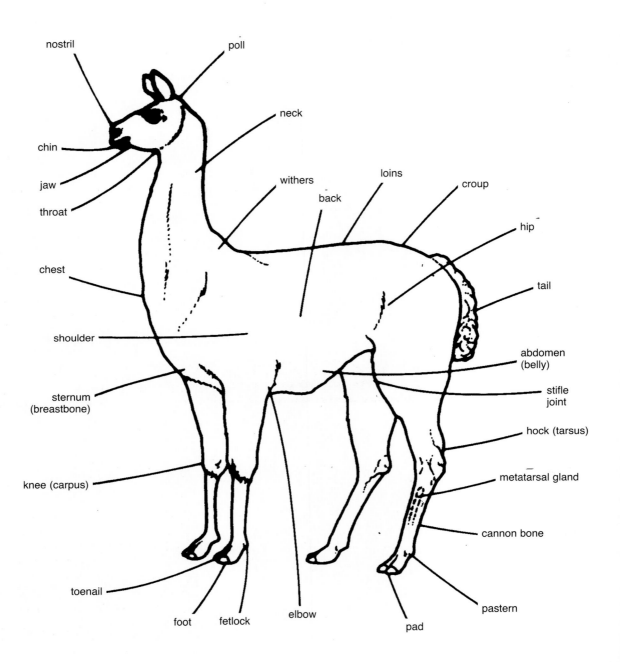

The points of the camelid.

A very fine-looking macho alpaca. Note the density and solid coverage of the fibre all over the body and down the legs. (Photo: John Gaye, Alpacas of Wessex)

Nice conformation. Note that short fleece gives an impression of longer neck and legs. What about the fleece though? It's the most important attribute of an alpaca.

Four offspring from a single superior male. Note their similarity to each other, indicating their father's highly desirable ability to consistently pass on his qualities to his offspring.

A line-up of progeny from another single elite sire. As with those above, the similarity in these animals illustrates the sire's ability to stamp his characteristics on his offspring. However, proper evaluation requires the inclusion of data from the dams of these animals. (Photo: John Gaye, Alpacas of Wessex)

You need to include both maternal and paternal measurements, or you won't be able to separate who is responsible for what you measure in the cria so accurately.

At present, little of this is done in camelids, and the practice of mating elite females with the best males means that the resulting high quality cria could be inheriting their excellence from either side. To get meaningful breeding value results, you do need the largest possible sample of offspring.

Breeding Value

This is the value assigned to a particular animal with respect to a particular physical characteristic, which indicates the likelihood of that animal's passing the characteristic on to its offspring. Breeding values are calculated using the data from as many progeny as possible, comparing the performance of the progeny with that of the parents with respect to the characteristic in question – for example, fleece weight or micron count at three years old.

LLAMA ASSESSMENT

There is a number of different types of llama, ranging from smaller, lighter animals to tall, rangy or large-boned ones. What are your requirements? If you wish to pack with your llamas, their fitness to carry loads and to walk long distances is important. If you want

Guanaco. This is the wild progenitor of the llama, and variations in this form represent directions taken by selective breeding. (Photo: Chris Eke, UK Llamas)

only pasture companions and pets, conformation matters only if it will affect the basic health of the animal.

Your considerations will be quite different if you are looking for a low-maintenance pair of pets from those if you want prize-winning breeding stock. Even if you do want to breed, be realistic about your goals with respect to your budget and the time you want to put into your animals. It is a very good idea to

131

A very pretty llama head. However, heads change shape as they mature; in particular, the nose will grow thicker. (Photo: Dick Hobbs)

Well-proportioned, mature llama head. (Photo: Chris Eke, UK Llamas)

have a checklist and award either ticks or points for everything on it, to make sure that you don't overlook anything. It is quite easy to be smitten by the eyes and completely forget to assess the rest of the animal!

Before going into a detailed examination of the animal, watch it move from a little distance. Do the limbs and body move straight, is it sound (i.e., not lame)? Observe it move from the front, towards you, from the rear, away from you and from the side. If possible have it move down a narrow walkway so that it must track a straight course, for at least 20m (22yd).

Llama Conformation

Head

The muzzle should be straight, the teeth meet the dental pad, the nostrils symmetrical, with

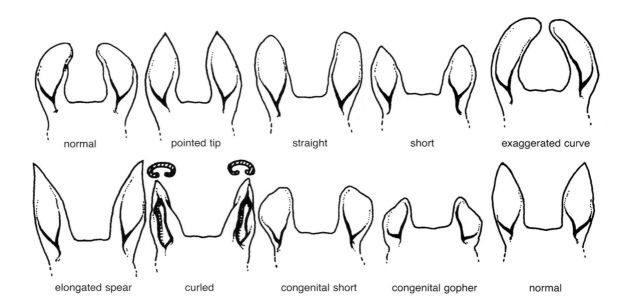

normal   pointed tip   straight   short   exaggerated curve

elongated spear   curled   congenital short   congenital gopher   normal

Possible ear defects in llamas. The basic form of the ears of the alpaca is given underneath. Resemblance to llama ears is taken as a fault in alpacas, since it may indicate crossbreeding with llamas in the animal's pedigree. The congenital faults might equally be seen in llamas and alpacas.

detectable air movement from both. The eyes should be clear and bright. There should be no discharges from eyes or nose, and the ears should not be bare or flaky. The ears should be the same length and shape, and curve inwards in the classic 'banana' shape. The edges should be smooth and meet evenly – beware of fused ear tips. The jaws should be symmetrical, without odd lumps or bumps. The head should be carried high when the animal is alert.

Many faults in conformation are inherited, so stock required for breeding should be scrutinized with the greatest care.

Neck
The neck should be straight, held vertically, and in proportion with the rest of the body.

Body
The topline should be horizontal and straight, and the rump fairly square, with the tail set high and carried slightly away from the body. The chest should be deep, with a pronounced rise up the belly to give a relatively narrow 'waist' in front of the hind legs. From the front, a broad chest should indicate a stronger animal with better stamina. Having said that, too round a body will tend to create instability under the pack. If you want the animal for packing, see it saddled and loaded. Condition score the animal. If it is not around 3–3.5 (on a scale of 0–5) ask yourself why. Obese animals can have problems as well as thin ones.

Legs
These should look fairly straight from the front and rear, with no deviations inside or out of the vertical line between the ground and the point where the legs join the body. Legs that are bent are more likely to become arthritic with age and wear, because there are inevitably uneven forces on different sides of the joint. Look at the profile diagrams on the next page and see how the legs should appear

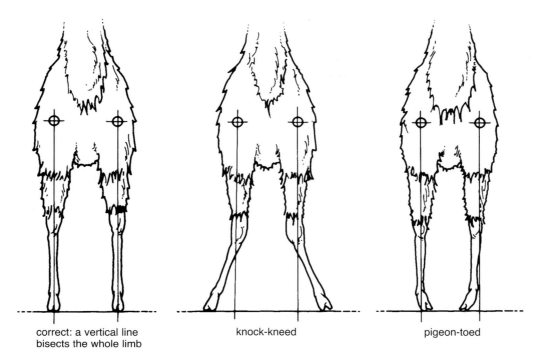

correct: a vertical line
bisects the whole limb

knock-kneed

pigeon-toed

Forelimb comformation.

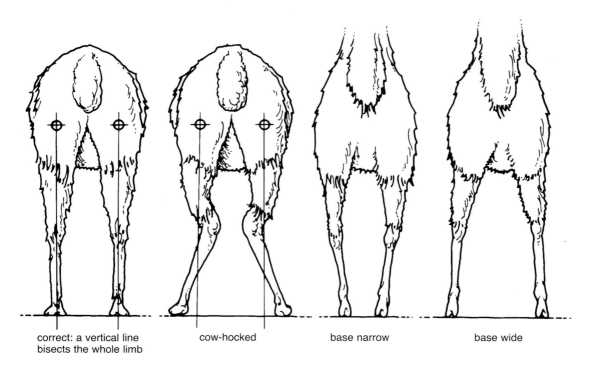

correct: a vertical line
bisects the whole limb

cow-hocked

base narrow

base wide

Hind limb conformation.

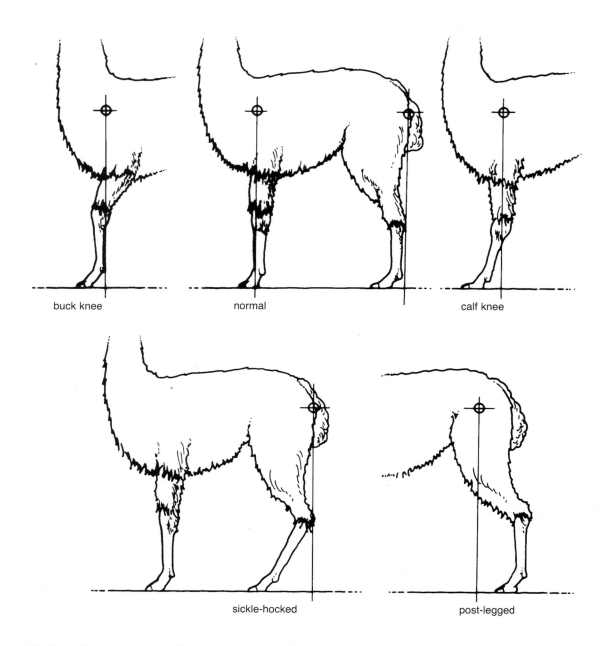

buck knee   normal   calf knee

sickle-hocked   post-legged

Limb conformation: animal viewed from the side.

when viewed from the side. If there is a great deal of fibre on the legs, have them wrapped so that you can see what form the bones take. Check the illustrations for some relatively common abnormal forms that you may see.

Feet

These should be of even size. If one is smaller than another it indicates a probable long-standing lameness. (The foot that is used the least will tend to shrink slightly.) The nails

136

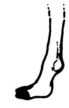

normal pastern

moderate hyperextension
of pastern

severe hyperextension
of pastern

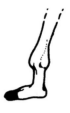

cocked ankle (contracted
flexor tendons of fetlock)

Conformation of the foot.

should be trimmed and the toes straight. The nails should be of roughly equal size, only two per foot, and properly separated from each other. (Fused toes and extra toes are both inherited defects.) The footpad should be smooth and have no signs of raggedness or defects. Check the pasterns for a reasonable degree of slope, avoiding hyperextension (*see* diagrams above).

Skin and Fleece

There should be no bare or flaky patches on the skin, apart from the 'scent glands' on the inner and outer surfaces of the cannon bones. At best, flakiness indicates a degree of ill-health or mineral deficiency; at worst it can be the early signs of intractable skin disease. The fibre should be growing evenly over the body, with no patches where it has fallen out.

Tail

Feel along the length of the tail through the fleece. It should be straight without kinks.

Genitalia

In females, the vulva must be clearly separated from the anus, and should open along its length. Deformities in this area are relatively common. In males, if entire, the testicles should be of even size, descended into the scrotum, but mobile within it, and of the correct size for the age of the animal (at least 2.5 × 4.5cm/1 × 1⅛in in the adult). If the animal is sexually mature, it should be possible

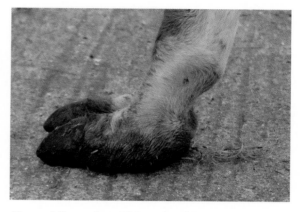

Normal llama foot. This animal is a pack llama whose feet rarely require trimming because they wear down in use.

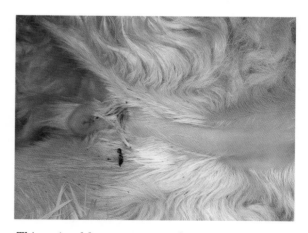

This animal has no anus, and faeces has exited from a fistula in the urethra, visible towards the left of the photograph. Deformities in this area are relatively common in llamas and alpacas.

ABOVE: *Prize-winning tampuli llamas, with their proud owner.*
LEFT: *Close-up on a winning head.*
(Photos: Chris Eke, UK Llamas)

to ease the penis out of the sheath (i.e. it should not still be attached to the sheath, as it is in immature males). If you are buying a young unproven animal for breeding, ask for a guarantee that it is fertile; reputable breeders who are charging a fair price for a breeding animal should agree to accept the animal back for a full refund if it fails to breed.)

In mature males, it is likely that the size of the testicles reflects the sperm count, and it is recommended that males with larger testicles be selected over equally good ones with smaller testicles. The sperm-count link is known to exist in other animals, and research in alpacas by David Pugh in America observed that males with bigger testicles (3.5×2.9cm)

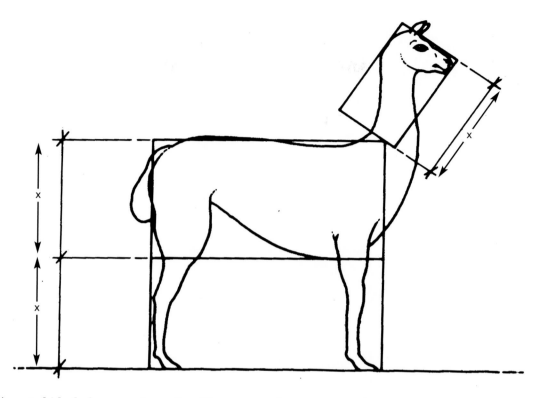

Accepted ideal alpaca conformation. These proportions vary considerably from those of the vicuna, the wild progenitor of the alpaca. There are no data on any practical benefits of these particular proportions.

achieved a higher impregnation rate than those with smaller ones (2.5 × 2.2cm). The first group got 70 per cent of females pregnant, while the second managed only 40 per cent. It is also true that males with larger testicles reach sexual maturity earlier, losing the attachments between the penis and the sheath, so that they become physically able to mate earlier.

ALPACA ASSESSMENT

See the animal moving, to make sure it moves straight, holds itself well and is not lame. If possible have it move loose (i.e. with no one leading it), down a narrow track so that it will go in a straight line, and watch it both approaching and going away from you, as well as from the side.

If you are looking for a cute grass-cutter, all that matters is that it is healthy and will fit in socially (and reproductively!) with your group. If you want to make more of a companion animal of it, and take it out for walks, then soundness and ability to move are more important. If you want a fibre-producing animal, the fleece is critical, as it is for a breeding animal, since with alpacas most of the value lies in the excellence of the fleece. However, you should still inspect the whole animal in a methodical way because problems not related to the fleece can still be important.

Alpaca Conformation

Head
The ears should be straight, spear-shaped and open properly along their length. Too-long ears

139

An ideal alpaca head, with a dense bonnet and blocky muzzle. (Photo: John Gaye, Alpacas of Wessex)

Heavily fibred alpacas can suffer from wool-blindness, where there is so much fleece on the face that they cannot see. Because heavy fibre cover is desirable, this is usually managed by trimming away the fibre from around the eyes. (Photo: Peter Watson, South West Alpacas)

tend to look llama-like, and – since we know that there has been interbreeding between alpacas and llamas – they are considered a fault. (There is still widespread interbreeding in South America, and the resultant crosses are termed 'huarizos' and 'mistis'.)

Be wary of scabby or scaly skin on the ears; it could represent a tendency to go on to develop skin disease. Refer to the llama pictures for possible congenital ear defects.

The 'bonnet' of fleece on the forehead should be rounded and dense, showing evidence of the crimp visible in the rest of the fleece. The animal should not have so much fleece around the eyes that it cannot see (so called 'wool blindness').

Eyes should be clear and bright, not blue, and with no discharges. They should be of symmetrical size and shape. (In the minds of some people, blue eyes are associated with deafness. There is a lack of good evidence that blue eyes predispose an animal to deafness, and deaf animals should be rejected for breeding regardless of the colour of their eyes. However, the association is likely to reduce the desirability of the animal to potential purchasers, and blue-eyed animals will usually command a lower price.)

The nose should be straight and slightly blocky in appearance. The nostrils should be clean, evenly sized and positioned. It should be possible to feel air moving in and out of each nostril. (A narrowing of the airway, restricting air movement here, is seen with the inherited congenital condition choanal atresia.) The face should look straight when viewed from the front.

The lips should be soft and free of blemishes. The teeth should meet the dental pad neatly. Check for fighting teeth.

Jaws should be even on both sides (i.e. symmetrical). Feel along them for any unusual swellings. A possible cause of swelling in the jaw is a tooth root abscess; these are relatively common and very difficult to treat.

Neck

The neck should be carried straight when the animal is alert. Head carriage is not as vertical as it is in llamas. The neck should be about as long, including the head, as the body is deep. The fleece on the neck should maintain the character of that on the blanket, and the area of guard hair on the chest at the base of the neck should be as small as possible.

Body

The topline in alpacas should be slightly rounded with a lower set tail, which is carried well away from the body only when the animal is excited. Flipping the tail over the rump indicates submission (described in

Most marks in the show ring are awarded for excellence of fleece. (Photo: John Gaye, Alpacas of Wessex)

Chapter 6). The overall shape of the body from the side should be as deep as the legs are long. The belly is normally less swept up than it is in llamas, and evidence of a round, deep, wide chest is somewhat less important since the animal's purpose is not to work. Nevertheless, the chest should not look narrow and pinched in from the front.

Genitalia

As with llamas, a female alpaca's vulva must be clearly separated from the anus, and should open along its length. It should be a minimum of 1cm (⅓in) long. Be suspicious of overlarge clitorises and vulval overdevelopment, since intersexes (i.e. a mixture of male and female because of genetic faults), do exist. Deformities in this area are relatively common.

As with llamas, the testicles of entire males should be of even size, descended into the scrotum, but mobile within it. They should be of the correct size for the age of the animal, i.e. greater than 3cm (1¼in) in the adult animal. In the adult male, as with lla-

mas, it should be possible to ease the penis out of the sheath. (If you are buying a young unproven animal for breeding, ask for a guarantee that it is fertile: reputable breeders charging a fair price for a breeding animal should agree to accept the animal back for a full refund if it fails to breed.) It is said that males with large testicles sire females who go on to milk well. I have not seen any data to confirm this, but, in other species, stud animals are expected and desired to have generously sized testicles.

Legs

These should be straight when viewed from the front and the sides, with the exception of the normal angles of stifle and hock. Neither of these should be excessively angled or straight. (*See* diagrams of limb conformation on pages 135–6). It is desirable for the legs to show coverage of fibre, even though, at present, this fleece is usually discarded. The convention is that the legs should be as long as the body is deep and as long as the head and neck together, but it is questionable whether this standard has any real productive relevance. Certainly the vicuna, the wild progenitor of the alpaca, has very much longer legs and neck, with a shallower body, than this convention. For a much fuller exploration of the variation of alpaca conformation with regard to that of vicuna, refer to Eric Hoffman's excellent work in *The Complete Alpaca*.

Angular limb deformities are common in alpacas. They usually affect the front legs, but the hind legs should also be checked for them. They occur when the middle joint of the front limb (the carpus, or knee) and the middle joint of the hind (the tarsus, or hock) is out of true with the upper limb and foot. Small defects are unlikely to have any effect on an individual, but larger ones are likely to make the animal prone to injury and/or arthritis as it ages.

Feet

These should be of even size, free of blemishes, with trimmed nails and straight toes. Check for any signs of disease between the toes, and for the correct number of toes (two for each foot!). Refer to diagrams of pastern conformation on page 137.

Tail

Feel this all along its length and ensure that it is free of lumps, bumps or kinks.

Fleece

Fleece assessment is covered in Chapter 7, and is the most important area of all. Well over half of the animal's value lies in the excellence of its fleece, and most of the marks in the showing ring are awarded for it.

SUGGESTED ASSESSMENT CHECKLIST

There are various screening lists available, all of which work on a similar principle. That is, by adopting a methodical and semi-quantitative approach, a consistent standard against which each individual animal can be assessed is achieved. The following checklist (on page 144)

is adapted from one originally designed by Eric Hoffman for screening imported alpacas. It is simplified to make it easier to use, although this renders it no longer suitable for import screening. Screening systems for import or registration should automatically eliminate animals that are severely affected by physical deformity. (For further information on international screening, refer to Eric Hoffman's original work for the Alpaca Registry Inc.)

SHOWING

Showing your animals can be very rewarding and enjoyable. The experience of going into a ring and having your stock compared with that of your colleagues is nerve-racking but, if you win a prize, hugely triumphant. It is also exciting and fascinating to see lots of animals belonging to other people and to have the opportunity to meet and talk to other camelid keepers.

If you wish to become a commercial success at llama or alpaca breeding, showing can be an important way of gaining widespread recognition of the superiority of your animals. Publicity and the opportunity to speak to potential customers, together with the opportunity for them to see your animals are all potential benefits of showing.

There is a certain risk entailed in showing. If your animals do not do well, you could destroy a potential market. Your prospects are dependent upon your ability to select quality animals to exhibit, on the judge's ability to recognize them, and on the chance that someone else will have something even better.

Preparation

If you are to show your animals, you want them to look their best. Since they are pasture animals, this can be harder to arrange than you might imagine. You will need a field that is clean, with no patches of mud in which they might roll, and free of vegetation such as brambles, burrs and seed heads, which will become tangled in the fleece. This is important if you are to keep the fleece in showing condition.

Checklist: Conformation

Identification of animal:
Age: Height:
Condition Score:

Head
From a maximum of 10 points, deduct points
for faults:

Head and muzzle:
1. Normal   0
2. Llama-like or alpaca-like*   up to –10
   (Note: If assessing llamas, deduct points for
   looking like an alpaca, if assessing alpacas,
   deduct points for looking like a llama.)
3. Overlarge/small   –2

Ears (*see* drawings of abnormal ear shapes)
1. Normal spear/banana shaped*   0
2. Asymmetric   –2
3. Incorrect shape   up to –15
                        (depending on severity)

Body Score (see *drawings of body scores*)
From an ideal 15 points deduct 20 points for
condition score 1, 15 points for condition score
5. Scores 2–4 inclusive are acceptable.

Legs and Balance
Straight correct legs score 15 points
1. Buck knees   (per affected leg) –5
2. Calf knees   (per affected leg) –7

3. Sickle hocks   (mild) –3
                                 (severe) –7
4. Cocked ankle (*see* diagram)   –20
5. Down on pasterns (*see* diagram)   –5
6. Post legged (too-straight legs)   front –2
                                      rear –5
7. Front view:
   Knock-kneed   (mild) –3
                              (moderate) –10
   Pigeon-toed   –5
   Base narrow   –3
   Base wide   –3
   Bow legged   –3
8. Rear view:
   Cow-hocked   (mild) –3
                              (moderate) –10
   Pigeon-toed   –5
   Bow-legged   –3
   Base narrow   –3

Legs, Body and Neck (see *diagram*)
1. Legs too long or short   –5
2. Neck too long or short   –5
3. Tail set (too high or low)   –5
4. Back (dipped or humped)   –5

Movement
Foot flight outside or inside footprints –7

Total from 40 available points: ___

Checklist: Fibre

Fleece Density (Huacaya)
Up to 15 points, unless very dense in which
case start from a maximum of 20 points. As
with conformation, points should be deducted
for faults.
1. Light fleece   –10
2. Average   –3
3. Dense   –0
4. Very dense   +5

Lustre and Curl (Suri)
Up to 15 points.
1. Absence of lustre   –7
2. Absence of curl   –8

Average Fibre Diameter (AFD)
Up to 15 points. Deduct 10 points for every
micron over 26. (1 point per 0.1 micron)

Standard Deviation (SD)
Up to 15 points. Deduct 5 points (or fraction pro
rata) for every 0.5 micron over maximum:

17 or less	Max SD = 4.0
17.1–19	Max SD = 4.5
19.1– 21	Max SD = 5.0
21.1–23	Max SD = 5.5
23.1 and over	Max SD = 6.0

Percentage of Fibres Over 30 Microns
Up to 15 points. Deduct 5 points for every percentage point over 5 per cent (e.g. 7 per cent
over 30 microns deduct 10 points)

Llamas in the show ring. This is where you get the chance to see the best on offer and to measure your judgement against that of the judges. (Photo: Chris Eke, UK Llamas)

It is possible to go to great lengths to groom and prepare llama fleeces, but alpaca fleeces are disturbed by grooming and the crimp will be lost. This will cause the animal to be marked down in the ring for lack of character and crimp of fleece, and should be avoided. It is common for larger breeders to trim off the guard hair from the surface of the fleece to improve the appearance, and make the guard hair harder for the judge to detect. I have always regarded this as bordering on the deceitful, but if your competitors are going to secure an advantage by doing it then you have to consider doing it too.

Training

Your animals will need to be halter trained and also accustomed to having themselves examined for assessment. Judges will quickly lose patience with owners whose animals will not stand still while they are assessed: they have a lot of animals to look at, and will not have the

145

Alpaca show – an excellent place to hone your assessment skills, even if you don't want to enter your own animals. (Photo: Jean Field, Devon Alpacas)

This is what the judges are looking for. (Photo: Peter Watson, South West Alpacas)

Once halter trained, even young animals can easily be managed by children under supervision, allowing the whole family to join in. (Photo: John Gaye, Alpacas of Wessex)

time to patiently administer a lesson in handling for you. Therefore make sure that any animals you wish to show are very used to being pulled, pushed, prodded and poked, and not unduly worried by it. Having companion animals in the pen is a must, but quiet, confident handling by the person they know and trust best will persuade most animals that there is really nothing to fear.

Attitude

Showing can be both exciting and a bit frightening for owners as well as for the animals. Concentrate on being calm and behaving normally around your animals, so as not to agitate them. If they misbehave, it will not be from mischief, but from confusion or fear, so they need to be reassured and encouraged, not reprimanded or threatened. Your demeanour will affect them, and if you are anxious, agitated or short tempered, they may well be nervous and upset.

Care of the Animals at the Show

Preparation is important. Think through the day, and what facilities the show will provide. The animals must have access to water and hay; where is it going to come from? Ideally,

Show Trade Stalls

These can be an important opportunity for potential customers to ask questions and to acquire information about your business as a whole, generating further marketing opportunities for you.

Breeder show stall displaying some of the goods that can be made from alpaca fleece. (Photo: Jean Field, Devon Alpacas)

The general public are drawn to alpaca and llama classes at shows, and shows provide an excellent opportunity to market your stock to enthusiastic people. (Photo: John Gaye, Alpacas of Wessex)

Almost as many people come to view the animals in their pens as watch the actual classes. (Photo: Jean Field, Devon Alpacas)

Show equipment. Most important are the hay and buckets for water. You will also need halters, lead ropes, brushes (for llamas), broom, rake, poo pot. And don't forget refreshments for the humans.

you will want a shady place for the animals to wait and rest. If you want to take food treats make sure that you limit the quantity consumed so as not to upset the digestion of already stressed animals; otherwise use harmless treats such as apple or carrot sticks. Think about the equipment you will need: have you enough buckets, haynets or bags, halters and lead-ropes? What about a container for some dung pellets to encourage them to relieve themselves when they get there, grooming tools for llamas, and a broom and rake to tidy up if necessary? Don't forget your paperwork – registration details of each animal to assist checking in, show timetable, a map to get you there, and some cash to make sure that the humans get fed and watered.

The Journey

How long will it take? Calculate your journey time with care. The last thing you need is to be rushing to get there in time when you are hauling a trailer of precious cargo. If the journey will take longer than a couple of hours, consider making a rest-stop somewhere, so that the animals can be unloaded, allowed to urinate and defecate, and offered water and hay. Take a plastic bag with some of their own droppings in it, so that these can be put down in an appropriate place to encourage them to 'go'. Some individuals are most reluctant to relieve themselves in a strange place where they feel threatened, and retaining urine especially for long periods can be very harmful.

CHAPTER 10

Breeding

Alpacas and llamas have a long gestation – being pregnant for approximately eleven months – and they almost always have only a single baby (cria). This reflects the marginal nature of the environment in which they evolved, where an individual animal is struggling to get enough food for its own needs, let alone those of young and growing offspring. In such a situation, trying to produce more young in a year would cause the death of both mother and baby through malnutrition or outright starvation. Reproductive patterns evolve over many generations, so our animals retain this defensive low level of reproductivity, even in the face of more than adequate nutrition.

FEMALE ANATOMY

Llamas and alpacas have a Y-shaped uterus, with almost all pregnancies being carried in the left horn. This means that eggs shed from the right ovary will have to migrate down the right horn to the body of the uterus and up the left horn if a successful pregnancy is to be established.

Hymen
This is a membrane, 3–4cm (1½–2in), which persists from embryonic development in maiden females. It can be quite tough to break down, and shy or unenthusiastic males can fail to achieve it. Mating will still stimulate ovulation and subsequent rejection of the male by the female but no pregnancy will result. It is common for vets or breeders to

use a sterile-gloved finger to break down the hymen of maidens for this reason.

MALE ANATOMY

Male alpacas and llamas have slim, almost worm-like penises, which point backwards when not erect. This means that they squat and urinate rearwards, much as the females do. When erect the penis does not really become any thicker, but is firmer, longer and points forwards. At the end of the penis is a firm projection: it is made of cartilage and has a slight curve in a clockwise direction. This helps the penis thread through the cervix, so that semen can be deposited directly into the uterine horns.

In newborn and juvenile males, the sheath of skin covering the penis adheres to it, so that it is impossible to extrude the penis to examine it. Only about 10 per cent of males have lost these by one year of age, about 70–80 per cent have by two years, and all should have done by three years. Since the loss of these adhesions is a sign of maturity, those males that lose them earlier should be expected to breed earlier. If the male should be castrated before the testosterone rush of the onset of puberty, then the adhesions may not break down completely. (Early castration may also delay the cessation of long bone growth, resulting in a rangy, post-legged animal, which can be at greater risk of joint problems.)

The scrotum of alpacas and llamas is situated just below the perineum, at the rear of

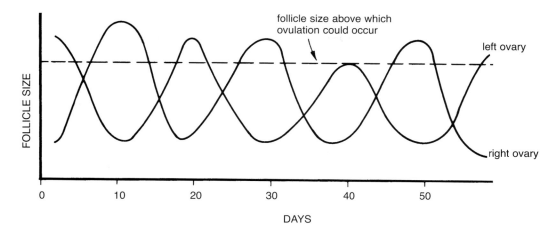

Diagram of variations in follicle size on each ovary. Follicular waves overlap every ten to twelve days to produce a follicle that is large enough to ovulate. However, there is considerable variation in length of cycle between individuals.

the body (as in cats) rather than under it between the hind legs, as in other domestic species. The testicles are oval in shape, and their size does give an indication of fertility, so larger testicle size is desirable. At one year of age, alpaca testicles should be at least 2–3cm (1in) long. They should have the consistency of a ripe tomato, and be freely mobile within the scrotum. The testicles will continue to enlarge in a breeding male to about 3.7 × 2.4cm in the alpaca, and 5.4 × 3.3cm in the llama.

Thorough examination of an animal intended for breeding, prior to purchase, is essential (*see* Chapter 9).

THE BREEDING CYCLE

Alpacas and llamas do not have oestrous cycles quite like most other domesticated animals who, as spontaneous ovulators, all produce eggs at more or less consistent intervals – within their breeding season if they have one – regardless of whether matings occur. Camelids are induced ovulators: they shed eggs only in response to mating. They do have what are called follicular waves, where an egg follicle will gradually mature to a point when it could be ovulated if mating occurred, and then regresses again if no mating takes place. All breeding cycles vary with individual animals, so timings are more of a general guide than a fixed rule, but female alpacas and llamas generally have follicular waves every ten to twelve days, with a few days in the middle of this cycle during which a follicle is mature enough to be ovulated if mating occurs, but not so old that it will turn into a corpus luteum without ovulating. A few individuals will ovulate spontaneously in the absence of mating.

As follicles mature, they produce a hormone called oestrogen, which causes receptive behaviour. Once they ovulate, they undergo a process called luteinization, and switch to producing progesterone, the hormone of pregnancy. While this is produced, the follicles are inhibited from development, and rejection behaviour is triggered. If there is no pregnancy, the uterus sends a signal to the ovaries and switches off the progesterone, allowing a new follicle to develop.

The overlapping nature of the follicular waves, and the fact that the female is receptive even if her follicle is not mature enough

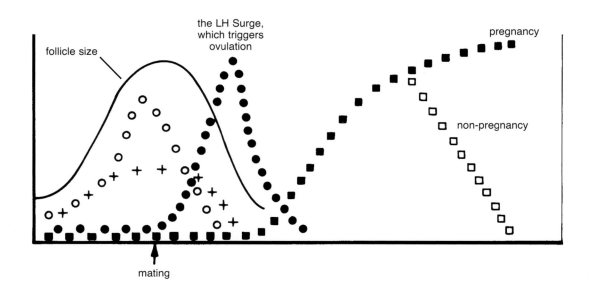

the LH Surge, which triggers ovulation

follicle size

pregnancy

non-pregnancy

mating

+ FSH (follicle-stimulating hormone)
o oestrogen
● LH (luteinizing hormone)
■ progesterone
□ progesterone (non-pregnancy)

Notes:
The LH surge occurs only after mating.
Progesterone levels wane if the mating was infertile.
High progesterone triggers rejection behaviour.
Progesterone rises only after ovulation and mating.

Hormonal fluctuations in association with follicular development and ovulation. This is a subtle system with positive and negative feedback loops that regulate and modify it. Its normal function depends upon general health and emotional state.

to ovulate (in fact she can 'sit' for the male at virtually any stage unless pregnant or recently mated) makes it very difficult to determine from behaviour alone when the best time to mate will be.

Ovulation

This is triggered by hormones released as a result of mating itself, and takes place twenty-four to forty-eight hours after the mating, where the female has a follicle sufficiently well developed to be capable of ovulation, and not so mature that it has lost the ability to ovulate. The sperm, which will have been ejaculated directly into the uterine horns, appear to be protected in the female tract while they

wait, in a gelatinous plug, which gradually liquifies over the intervening hours.

MATING

First Mating

In South America, females are not mated until they have attained a bodyweight of 33kg (about 70lb); 70 per cent of these maiden females will become pregnant. It should be remembered that in South America, animals are generally on poorer diets and thinner, so this weight would be associated with an older animal and larger frame size than would usually be the case in the UK. Interestingly,

The normal mating position for both alpacas (pictured) and llamas. (Photo: Karen Oglesby, Meon Valley Alpacas)

according to research done in South America, mating and pregnancy does not appear to stunt continued growth when these mated yearlings are compared with females that have not been bred from.

In practice, in Britain, mating females at around a year of age as long as they are well grown and nourished, seems to result in acceptable levels of fertility and health for both mother and cria.

Once calved, the female will become receptive to the male again at two to three weeks, and as long as the pregnancy and birth have not caused any damage to her, may well conceive again if mated at that time.

Paddock Mating

With this system of management, the male is left to run with the females and mates them when he determines. It requires much less human time and intervention, but precise calving dates will not be known.

Hand- or Pen Mating

These are terms used to describe the practice of supervised mating, where a non-pregnant female is put into a pen with a male while mating takes place, and then returned to a paddock without males, so that both the timing of the mating and the only possible sire of the cria are both known.

The other advantage of this type of mating is that very valuable males do not waste their energies repeatedly mating the same female, and can be used to impregnate more females as a result. The disadvantage of this type of mating management is that much time can be wasted if receptive but non-fertile females are presented for mating. When the male is with a herd of females, he can determine the best time for mating and immediately mate the most receptive females.

Stud Services

If you own your own stud male, you can expect him to serve up to forty to sixty females per year. Unless your enterprise is very large, you effectively have 'free' matings and can use him to suit yourself.

Stud Farms

These are farms that have stud males as a major source of income, selling services to breeders who do not own a stud male, or who want to use a particular male for a particular female. At the time of writing it is possible to pay anywhere between £100 and £2,000 for a service, depending on the popularity of the stud male concerned. The usual terms are that the amount is only payable for a live cria that survives a certain number of hours after birth, although it is usual to pay once the female is confirmed pregnant (usually by ultrasound examination) and to have subsequent matings at no extra charge should she abort.

Various arrangements can be reached with stud owners. Some will keep your female on their farm and tease and mate her until they are satisfied that she is pregnant. This process may take up to three months, and some owners are unwilling to pay the boarding (also called agistment) fees for this length of time. Alternatives are taking the female to the stud farm, having her mated immediately, and then taking her home again, or having the male visit the female's farm, mate her, and then return immediately to his own farm (so called 'drive by' matings).

If an owner of females has a sufficient number to mate, a stud male owner may be willing to allow his male to go to the females' farm until they are all pregnant, or hire or lease a male for a season.

The Mating Process

When put with a receptive female, the male will approach with tail held high, and head and neck extended towards her. She should tolerate his approach, although she may move away. If she lays back her ears and spits, she is rejecting his advances. He will start to 'orgle' – the special guttural call of the male while mating. She may kush immediately or when he mounts her, but should go down fairly readily if she is receptive. He then positions himself tucked tightly over her hindquarters, with his forelimbs clasped about her chest, and begins to mate her, orgling constantly. Mating may well take half an hour or longer, and one or both animals may shift slightly. Sometimes the female lies down with her head outstretched, and occa-

sionally goes over onto her side. Sometimes the male will dismount, reposition himself, and begin again. Occasionally he will get up and move away before recommencing.

Rejection

Typically the female spits vigourously at or past the male to discourage his approach. Often this is sufficient. Experienced stud males are often insistent, though, and if she has space, a non-receptive female may run from him. Receptive females may run initially but then allow themselves to be caught after a short chase. Males are frequently uninterested in non-receptive females and, if put with a group of females, may sniff them in turn and ignore non-receptive ones. (However, it has been observed that when alpaca males are left with a group of females, although they may mate several in a day for the first few days, after about two weeks they ignore even newly receptive females.)

Rejection behaviour is triggered by high progesterone levels in the female, and if she has a persistent corpus luteum (this occurs if the signal from a non-pregnant uterus fails to break it down) she will continue to reject the male even though not pregnant.

Timing of Mating

For breeders who do not own a stud male, avoiding unnecessary trips to the stud farm or visits from the stud male is desirable. Timing matings so that a pregnancy is most likely to result is important to avoid wasting any of the resources involved, be they time in gestation, human time, effort and expense, or stud male energy and sperm supply.

The usual procedure with a female that we wish to get pregnant is to present her to the male. If she is empty, she will be expected to sit and accept a mating. Following mating, we expect her to reject the male, by running if she has space, or spitting and spinning about, refusing to go down. Unless she had an immature follicle at mating, and did not therefore ovulate, this will happen for a minimum of five to six days, but immature follicles continue to mature and she may accept a further mating in two to three days' time, at which she will ovulate. If the follicle that was present when she was mated was too mature, it won't have ovulated, but will still luteinize and the luteal phase (*see* diagram on page 152) that follows is quite short. If ovulation took place, then the normal progesterone-dominated luteal phase of ten to twelve days follows. If there is no pregnancy, then a new follicular wave proceeds, and under the influence of oestrogen the female becomes receptive again.

With these general guidelines on normal timing in mind, it makes sense to tease a female from three to six days following a mating. If she rejects, then teasing her at ten to twelve days in case there was an ovulation but no pregnancy is wise. If a journey to the putative sire is involved, having a teaser male animal so that receptivity can be established at home is very useful, although management of this must be secure enough to ensure that there will not be an unwanted mating.

The complications of timing mating really revolve around the problem of the female being receptive at times when she has no fertile egg to ovulate. If the follicle is too immature, then she will remain receptive after mating; if too mature, then a short period of rejection follows mating and, if just right, then a longer period before returning to receptivity if no pregnancy has resulted.

PREGNANCY DIAGNOSIS

Rejection Behaviour
In the first instance, rejection of the male is the usual means of indicating that conception may have taken place. However, this is not wholly reliable because persistent corpus luteum – where the mechanism that causes the corpus luteum to break down fails in the non-pregnant animal – can be a cause of continued rejection by a non-pregnant female.

Ultrasound Scanning
It is possible to visualize a pregnancy with an ultrasound scanner from only few days after

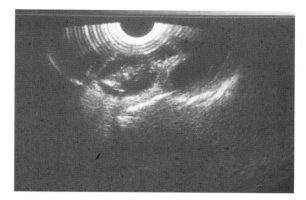

Ultrasound scan of an alpaca's uterus in early pregnancy. Below the bright white curved area at the top of the scan, a double black round area is visible, corresponding with the two horns of the fluid-filled uterus. The white shape in the left-hand horn is an embryo.

conception, but for these early scans a rectal probe must be used. This procedure is often resented by the female, and since a wrestling match is the last thing a newly pregnant animal needs, this is rarely practised.

More commonly, the female will be scanned using a transabdominal probe (one that is merely laid on the surface of the abdomen, high up on the hairless area near the udder) from about twenty-eight days onwards.

Ultrasound scanning is the most reliable method of diagnosing pregnancy and can be highly accurate, but it should be remembered that around 10 per cent of established pregnancies fail, so that a positive scan does not guarantee a live cria.

Blood Testing
Blood tests to measure progesterone levels have been used in llamas and alpacas, but the level of progesterone required to maintain a pregnancy seems to be very variable, with crias being born to dams with very low levels of progesterone in the blood stream. This variability makes the blood test unreliable.

Rectal Examination
Manual palpation of the uterus through the rectal wall has been done, but is impractical

for small females or operators with large hands, and suffers from similar problems to those of rectal probe ultrasound.

Foetal Heartbeat

Specialist listening devices such as Sonicaid can detect a foetal heartbeat from around ten weeks of pregnancy, and if used at this stage are 80–90 per cent accurate. As the foetus enlarges and slides forward and down into the abdomen, it becomes more difficult to locate the heartbeat accurately.

CONCEPTION FAILURE

There are various reasons why, after an apparently normal mating, the female llama or alpaca fails to become pregnant. The most obvious, perhaps, is infertility, which is dealt with in the next section. However, where infertility as a cause has definitely been eliminated, one of the following may be the reason:

- Mistiming of mating.
  Mating has not occurred when female is in the fertile phase of her cycle, even though receptive. (*See* above.)

- Incomplete mating.
  It is possible for less experienced males not to succeed in getting into the female properly, or even at all. So during the mating it's a good idea just to get down on your hands and knees and to check that everything is where it should be. Since mating commonly takes over half an hour, and always takes many minutes, there is plenty of time to do this.

- Persistent hymen.
  In some maiden females the hymen is so tough that the male does not succeed in penetrating it. For a pregnancy to result, he needs to deposit the semen right into the uterus. The hymen can be manually broken down by a breeder or vet using a sterile gloved finger.

INFERTILITY

This is a huge subject in itself, and there are many possible causes of infertility, ranging from management failure, through congenital deformity and infection to nutritional deficiency. Infection in the male or female reproductive tract can cause infertility or early loss of the embryo or foetus. Where males are used on a large number of females from different farms, they are at risk of catching and spreading infections. Many nutrients are vital for proper reproductive function, and lack of one or more can cause pregnancies either to fail to be established, or to fail early.

Your strategy should be to provide optimum care, management and nutrition for your animals. Have you carried out a basic breeding soundness examination? If they still fail to breed, then it's time to call the vet, since specialist examination and sampling may be needed to assess the conditions of the uterus and ovaries.

Female Infertility

If a female is failing to become pregnant then the possibilities are:

- Failure of ovulation.
  Possible causes for this are malformed or non-functional ovaries, hormonal abnormalities, mating when follicle is not mature.

- Failure of fertilization.
  This may be the result of poor quality eggs, obstruction of the Fallopian tube, poor quality sperm, infection, or mistimed mating.

- Failure of implantation.
  Uterine scarring, progesterone deficiency and infection are the major causes of implantation failure. These are dealt with in the next section on pregnancy loss.

Male Infertility

This can be a temporary phenomenon – if the weather has been very hot, or he has mated too many other females recently. If the male is not proven (i.e. has not definitely sired crias in the past) he may have some permanent problem.

A systematic approach to male infertility will help direct efforts to solve the problem most usefully. The first thing to detemine is whether or not he is physically normal. A breeding soundness examination should include watching him move, to see that he's physically fit enough to chase and mount females, palpation of his testicles to see that they are normal (*see* Chapter 9), and examination of the penis to see that it can emerge from the sheath and is normal.

Possible causes of male infertility are: overuse (too many matings in a short time), heat stress, infection, old age, debility, infirmity, hormonal failure, physical deformity, failure to mate.

PREGNANCY LOSS

It is thought that roughly 10 per cent of pregnancies fail between conception and birth. Often only individual females are affected and equally often no definitive diagnosis is ever made.

Early failure is most common, and with early embryonic death, often the affected females will not even have been diagnosed pregnant, but will have become receptive to the male again after having initially 'spat off'. It is only really possible to be sure that a pregnancy has been lost (rather than failed to conceive) if the animal has been diagnosed pregnant by ultrasound. Behaviour, i.e. 'spitting off' is about 85 per cent accurate.

The causes of pregnancy loss divide into infectious, nutritional, genetic and environmental.

Infectious Agents

Any severe infection or illness may result in abortion or early embryonic death, simply by debilitating the mother sufficiently.

Infectious agents that can cause abortion storms in an affected herd include *Chlamydia*,

Toxoplasma, *Leptospira*, and *Brucella*. In addition, other bacteria can occasionally cause an infection and inflammation of the placenta, leading to abortion, most frequently when there is some predisposing cause, like poor conformation of the vulva, or prolapsed vagina during pregnancy.

If a female is known to have aborted, then the foetus and placenta should be submitted to a laboratory for diagnostic samples without delay. In the time taken for it to get there, it should be cooled (not frozen). For some conditions a swab from the female's vagina and or a blood sample may also be required.

Any discharge from the vulva of a female who repeatedly fails to maintain a pregnancy should be swabbed to check for infection.

Nutritional Causes

Selenium, Vitamin A and iodine have all been associated with pregnancy loss when deficient. Vitamin A and iodine seem more likely to affect younger females, perhaps because they are still growing. In other species other deficiencies, such as zinc, are also related to poor fertility. Females who are lactating are more prone to pregnancy loss from nutritional deficiency, because they are already using nutrients for milk production.

At the other end of the nutritional spectrum, excess nutrition and obesity causing hepatic lipidosis (*see* earlier section on digestive diseases) can result in disturbances in body chemistry, which cause pregnancy loss.

Environmental Causes

The most common of these is stress, and there are many stressors that can be responsible. Handling for husbandry procedures, transport, heat, attack by dogs and bullying are all possible causes. One female being imported was held up by an officious individual at the airport and left in her crate for hours. She aborted, and then, still crated so that she could not move about, went on to prolapse her uterus. It seems that these animals can tolerate short periods of stress fairly well, but prolonged anxiety and agitation cause them to suffer.

Uterine prolapse. This follows calving and is a surgical emergency: call the vet immediately. (Photo: Tom Chamberlain)

Repaired prolapse. The stitches were removed after about two weeks. (Photo: Tom Chamberlain)

The patient feeding her new baby. She recovered uneventfully, but may have difficulty carrying a further pregnancy if there was much damage to the organ. (Photo: Tom Chamberlain)

Drug Reaction

Some drugs cause pregnancy loss. The prostaglandins should never be used in females that may be pregnant unless an abortion is desired, since they reliably end pregnancy by destroying the corpus luteum.

Corticosteroids, which may be administered for other reasons, can cause abortion.

Vaccination has occasionally been associated with abortion in some individuals. It is thought to be more of a problem where multivalent vaccines (i.e. vaccines against many different strains) are used.

Hormone Deficiency

This is environmental in the sense that the environment inside the female is wrong. For some reason (almost always unknown) she fails to produce sufficient progesterone to maintain the pregnancy, even though she has a corpus luteum. It is difficult definitively to diagnose, because some females seem to be able to carry pregnancies to term on extremely low levels of progesterone. Treatment with slow release progesterone implantation can be attempted, but monitoring of the pregnancy is vital, since the artificial hormone may cause the female to retain a non-viable pregnancy instead of aborting the dead foetus.

Uterine Scarring

A female that has sustained damage to her uterus from a very bad calving, prolapse or infection, may not be able to implant and maintain a pregnancy. A period of sexual rest and appropriate treatment to ensure that no infection remains in the uterus can sometimes help.

Cervical Incompetence

This is the inability of the cervix to remain closed during pregnancy. (A closed cervix is of course essential for retaining the foetus in utero.) The condition is most likely to occur in the female that has had calving difficulties that have damaged her cervix, which is then unable to remain closed in future pregnancies.

Genetic Causes

Twinning frequently causes late term abortion, as the placenta struggles to provide adequate nourishment for two foetuses. Twin conceptions often self-reduce to singles early on in gestation. But there is some argument for terminating those that do not spontaneously abort, since there is a very high likelihood that both foetuses will be lost late on in pregnancy, usually wasting a year of the mother's breeding life. Nevertheless, healthy viable twins are occasionally born at term.

Severe foetal malformations can result in abortion on rare occasions, although, in general, pregnancy seems to have a way of recognizing malformed embryos early on, and losing them at the early embryonic death stage. Indeed, it has been speculated that one of the causes of early embryonic loss may be this mechanism in action.

EMBRYO TRANSFER AND ARTIFICIAL INSEMINATION

Research is being carried out on the use of embryo transfer, where multiple embryos are created in a single superior female, then individually transplanted into inferior females. These inferior females then bear and raise a cria to whom they are not genetically related. The advantage of this strategy is that you can multiply the genes of superior females without having to rely on her own reproductive function, and her limitation of around ten to fifteen crias over a lifetime of breeding. It also means that you can use the inferior female for what she does best – pregnancy and lactation – without being encumbered with her poorer qualities in her offspring. There are already alpacas in the UK that have been bred using embryo transfer.

Artificial insemination has the advantage that you can transport semen, rather than animals, and therefore reduce the costs and health problems involved. However, it has proved difficult to find extenders that keep camelid semen potent and usable. It has a tendency to turn to gel after ejaculation, making it technically impossible to use. If research succeeds in solving these problems, the stress of transporting animals for matings could theoretically, in the future, be largely avoided.

SELECTION OF BREEDING STOCK

Before embarking on a breeding programme, it is important to realize that breeding is a demanding undertaking. Animals used for breeding require far more resources in terms of nutrition, fencing, shelter, pasture space, time and money than bachelor herds of castrated or entire males.

Having decided to commit to the responsibilities involved, you need to decide your objectives: it is all very well to know how to manage matings, but the question of which animals to mate with which is altogether more difficult. The first question you need to answer is, 'What kind of animals do you want to produce?'

Pet-Quality Animals

These are usually attractive, coloured animals for the pet/park animal market. Such individuals are destined to spend their lives as attractive lawn mowers, with a varying degrees of interaction with their owners. The qualities they require are robust basic health and appealing looks. Stamina, in the case of llamas, or fleece quality in the case of alpacas, will not be important, but temperament will be. Niceties of conformation are not very important as long as the animals are sufficiently well put together not to be prone to health problems.

In practice, most of the animals who fall into this useful and popular category, are rejects from more exalted stock, who fail to meet the standards of conformation, colour, and quality to qualify as potential breeding animals.

Production Stock

These are animals suitable for use in the end objectives for their type. For llamas these will be trekking or flock guardian animals, frequently neutered, who will spend much of their lives usefully employed carrying packs for walkers or protecting flocks, usually of sheep, and occasionally of poultry. Pack animals need to be well-built, strong, and capable of becoming fit and developing endurance in work. A tractable, co operative temperament is essential, since animals who misbehave in a strange place can be a hazard to life and limb, quite apart from ruining what is supposed to be a pleasant leisure activity for the people involved. Guardian animals need to have the correct temperament to adopt and care for their flock. Outright aggressiveness is not of itself a necessary or sufficient qualification.

With alpacas, production animals are kept for their fleece. This will be shorn annually or in some cases every two years, and sold for processing. At the time of writing it is difficult to build a commercial enterprise around the sale of raw alpaca fleece. There is as yet minimal demand for it, and only a handful of processing enterprises willing to buy it. Prices paid do not cover production costs, except in the case of selling fleece directly to hand spinners, who pay significantly more for individual fleeces. However, it is likely that as the number of the national herd increases sufficient fibre will be produced to make industrial production of British alpaca products economically feasible, and a market can be built up. When this happens, herds of animals kept for the primary purpose of providing raw fleece become a possibility. These animals will need to have been bred to produce the maximum possible quantity of the best possible quality fleece. Minor conformation faults will be less important. Resistance to disease and parasites will also be valuable, and, most importantly, the ability to retain fleece quality over a lifetime, and not to 'blow out' into coarse, low value, fleece as the animals age.

Breeding Stock

These animals should embody all the ideal qualities for their production purposes, but to a greater degree, so that their offspring will be likely to reflect those qualities. Minor faults become more important, since they will

Three elite male alpacas. Note the dense, heavy-looking fibre on all of them, and also the differences in conformation between them in terms of leg and body length, degree of fibre on head, straightness of leg. All are champions, but each would balance slightly different qualities in a female. (Photo: John Gaye, Alpacas of Wessex)

have an effect in the animal's offspring. With females, who will have only about ten to twenty offspring in a lifetime, this is a little less important, but males can have that many in a season, so their faults and virtues are critical. Remember that mothering and milking ability are important female traits, as are libido and fertility in the male. (*See* Chapter 9 on selection of breeding animals, and for further information on the importance of genetics as well as looks.)

Individual qualities can be very valuable; for instance the ability to retain fleece quality throughout life in alpacas, or soundness of temperament or limbs in llamas. The animals who possess those qualities may therefore be desirable breeding stock – even though they also have faults – because they provide an opportunity to advance the degree of the favourable characteristic in your herd. When choosing their mates, you should seek to balance any faults they possess by selecting an animal that is particularly good in the area that its mate is weak.

GENETIC INHERITANCE

When animals are bred together, the qualities that are expressed in the young are largely a matter of chance. Just as it is possible to get

Who's your Daddy? Colour inheritance in llamas and alpacas is complicated and can be difficult to predict. (Photo: Karen Oglesby, Meon Valley Alpacas)

crias who will be better than either parent, it is also possible to get ones that are worse than either. Certain characteristics are genetically dominant, and therefore more likely to be expressed, but because they can hide the possession of the recessive gene for the less desirable characteristic, it is still possible to be unlucky. There are no real certainties in genetic selection, just probabilities. It is important to bear this in mind when considering what to pay for stud services: you are guaranteed a live cria, but not necessarily one that will be the same as its father.

Colour

Colour inheritance in llamas and alpacas is complicated. There are many different colour patterns and shades, with a complex system of dominant, incompletely dominant, recessive and restrictive genes. It appears possible for colour patterns to be hidden by recessiveness for generations, only to pop up where least expected.

Llamas can be any colour and still fulfil their primary purposes, but if alpacas are to produce industrial quantities of processible fleece, they really need to be white or extremely pale. Despite this, keepers of alpacas are attracted by coloured animals, and therefore the breeding of coloured animals remains commercially viable. Indeed, for those animals destined to be pets and pasture ornaments, an attractive appearance is much more important than fleece quality.

CHAPTER 11

Birth

Once you have established that an animal is pregnant, you will need to ensure that she receives the correct diet for her condition (*see* Chapter 4). As the time for birth approaches, you can reduce the chances of anything going wrong by taking the following precautions:

1. Know when the cria is due.
   You can then keep a close eye on the mother and be ready to act if she has any trouble. This is obviously easier with hand- rather than paddock mating.

2. Don't upset heavily pregnant females.
   You are more likely to get normal births with relaxed, healthy (and that does not mean overfat), undisturbed mothers. It is unwise to move them about close to calving because they need to feel confident about their territory so that when they move away from the herd to calve, they know they are moving to a safe area. Handling for husbandry purposes should be avoided if at all possible (it's not always possible), especially with individuals who get very upset by it. As the time for the birth draws near, don't keep approaching if you think a female is going into labour. She wants to be alone: use binoculars until you are sure she really needs you.

3. Know your female's normal behaviour.
   Spend time observing your animals' normal behaviour. Just about all calving females will behave differently from their normal routine as they start to go into labour; if you know what is normal for your female, then you will be alerted when things start to happen.

Alpacas and llamas usually deliver a single cria after about eleven calendar months of gestation. The process of birth is very similar to calving in cattle, foaling in horses or lambing in sheep.

LABOUR

First Stage
As with all natural processes, there is a large amount of variation within the range of what is normal. First-stage labour, during which the uterus is beginning to contract to push the foetus towards the birth canal, and the cervix is relaxing, can last from two to six hours. It probably won't be apparent to a watching human unless he or she knows the animal very well; the female will appear more restless, may hum more, will urinate and defecate repeatedly. The mother will usually absent herself from her group, so you may spot her away from them, on her own. After a variably brief period of restlessness, the move into second-stage labour will begin.

Second Stage
Stage two is the pushing stage during which the baby is delivered; some fluid will appear at the vulva, and possibly a bag of birth fluid, the amnion. There will be a bulging of the

Look carefully: she is on her own and second-stage labour has already begun.

She's down and looking uncomfortable.

The audience is getting interested.

perineum, and the head, feet and front legs of the cria will appear.

The mother will continue to strain and deliver her baby front feet first, followed by the head, shoulders and the rest of its body. She may remain standing throughout the process, or lie down, and she may, if lying, get up and turn over. A normal delivery is quite swift, lasting from about five to twenty minutes. The photographs on this and the following two pages illustrate the progress of second-stage labour.

Getting up and down is common during labour.

Easy does it; the cria is correctly presented with both front feet and head visible. Watch from a distance and don't disturb her. It is normal for the feet to appear above the head of the baby.

There is still definite progress, and no need to intervene.

When the new arrival touches down, the mother will not lick it, so approach quietly and check that it's OK. If the weather is good, retire and wait for it to get to its feet to feed. Usually the rest of the herd will come to inspect the new member.

The umbilical cord should separate naturally 15–20cm (6–8in) from the cria's abdomen, with little bleeding, as the cria drops to the ground, or as the mother rises after giving birth lying down. The normal weight range of an alpaca cria is 6–10kg (13–22lb); a llama one is 8–20kg (18–44lb). As with other species, very small babies are at greater risk of dying in the first days of life, and very large ones are associated with greater difficulties in labour.

Up and following its mother, this cria has got off to an ideal start.

Feeding. The next vital hurdle; the new baby must take milk within twenty-four hours, and will do much better if it manages to do so within twelve hours – the sooner the better. (Photos, pages 164–7: Karen Oglesby, Meon Valley Alpacas)

If the female chooses to deliver standing, the natural pause between delivering the shoulders and the hips allows fluid to drain out of the lungs and airways. Note the shiny appearance of the epidermal membrane which covers the cria, a normal feature of camelid newborns. (Photo: Peter Watson, South West Alpacas)

It is not uncommon for a female to give birth while lying down. The advantage is that the cria does not bruise its head as she moves about; the disadvantage is that the fluids do not drain from the chest and airways so effectively. (Photo: Peter Watson, South West Alpacas)

ABOVE *Normal alpaca placenta (afterbirth) delivered inside out.*

RIGHT *Normal llama placenta delivered right way out, with whiter surface showing. Some normal birth fluid is still present. (Photos: Dick Hobbs)*

Third Stage

After the cria is born, stage-three labour, when the placenta is delivered, should occur within two hours. If this stage takes longer than six hours, it is considered abnormally long. If the placenta does not pass within twenty-four hours, call your vet.

The placenta should be inspected for completeness. Usually it is delivered inside out, and looks reddish in colour, and slightly rough on the surface. Occasionally it will be reversed, when it is whitish and smoother looking. It is crescent shaped, with the pattern of both uterine horns visible.

The mother does not attempt to eat the placenta, as with some species, and if left in the field it will attract foxes or other vermin, so it should be disposed of. The placenta is also called the afterbirth, or the cleansing. Females are said to have cleansed.

HOW TO SPOT TROUBLE

Abnormal behaviour is always the key indicator that an animal is in difficulties. As stated above, knowing the normal behaviour for your animals is vital if you are going to notice when things are going wrong for them. A

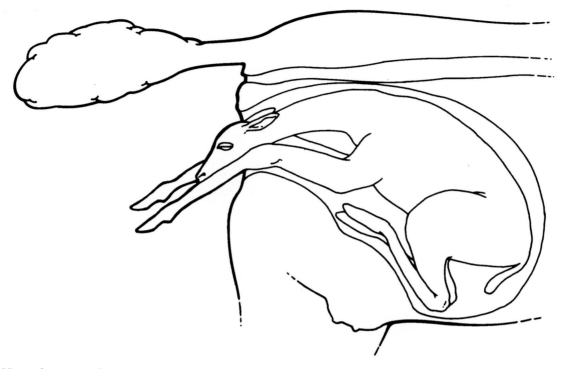

Normal presentation.

female who has moved away from the herd, who is not either chewing the cud or grazing, who gets up and lies down repeatedly, or who seems to be squatting and straining very frequently, is probably in labour – if she is due; if she is not due, she probably has colic.

INTERVENTION

Although there are rare exceptions, alpacas and llamas tend to give birth early in the day, and certainly before mid-afternoon. If you notice a female in trouble late in the day, the chances are that she has been in labour since the morning, and you have limited time left in which to help: it's an emergency. Even the best vet in the world cannot be everywhere at once, so the object of this section is to give you some clues about how you can help if veterinary assistance is not minutes away.

Once you have satisfied yourself by discreet observation that your female is in labour, carry on watching her for half an hour. She should have made visible progress in this time, if not delivered her cria. Remain at a distance that causes her no disquiet during this time, so as not to upset the smooth progress of her efforts. If there is no progress, then you need to investigate.

The cria should be born front first, right way up (i.e. with head above feet) with the two front feet pointing forward, straight, preceding the nose through the birth canal. You may well be able to correct minor malpresentations so that the cria can be born, and also help a tired female who has run out of 'push'.

Rules of Engagement

1. Be calm!
   The last thing the female in labour needs is stress, so keep calm, and speak to her and handle her gently, especially if she is uncooperative, which indicates that she is afraid.

Equipment

If you are to assist at a calving, you will need some basic equipment:

- Obstetric gloves. Gloves are important as they increase the cleanliness with which you

can assist a delivery and provide the animal with some protection from fingernails. Surprisingly, they have very little adverse effect on dexterity once you are inside the animal. They must be stored in very clean conditions, obviously.

- Obstetric lubricant. Lubrel and J Lube (*see* photograph below) are two common obstetric lubricants. Lubrel is a liquid, while J Lube is a powder that sticks to your glove and produces a slippery covering on contact with water. Lard can work well enough in an emergency.

- Clean, boiled (i.e. sterilized) calving ropes or lambing tapes. These are extremely useful to hold a limb or head while you manipulate the rest of the cria. Ideally they should be of different colours: I use a 'Red for Head' code, so as not to be confused about which piece of anatomy I am pulling.

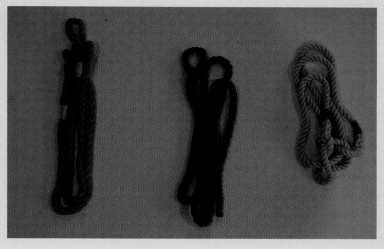

2. Be clean!
   Wash hands, and use the long plastic gloves (these reduce friction as well as increase cleanliness) and lubricant (you can lay in a small store from your vet before your crias are due). Don't lean on the ground or the animal with a hand that you then put inside her. Get her to the cleanest possible location or bring clean straw to put down (bearing in mind her need to be within sound and sight of her herd or at least a companion animal) before you begin.

3. Be gentle!
   If you are brutal or clumsy, it is quite possible to injure either the cria or the mother, so treat all soft tissues like wet Kleenex.

Correctly placed calving rope with loop placed centrally in the direction of pull. Pulling on this rope will not cause the loop to tighten and strangle the cria.

Incorrectly placed rope. Placement of the loop to one side of the direction of pull causes it to tighten when pulled.

4. Be small!

There is not much space in there, and if your hands resemble prize hams with ten sausages attached, this is not for you: find someone smaller to do the manipulations.

Common Malpresentations

These include: one or both feet back; fetlock (lowest leg joint) knuckled; knee(s) bent; head back. These are theoretically simple to correct as long as everything else is normal. Insert a clean, gloved, lubricated hand, follow the presented head or leg to the trunk, locate the turned back limb or head, and gently manipulate straight. Be very patient when you manipulate, things are often slippery, and it may take several attempts to arrange them as you want them. Wiggle your closed

fingers very slightly and gently, as you advance them, to push tissues and membranes out of your way. Keep your hand sliding up the bit of the baby you can feel, to stay inside its birth sac. Always retrieve a missing limb by working down it from the trunk so that you know it's from the right end of the right baby. (Twins are rare in alpacas, but who would want to be caught out?) Once you find the end of the limb, keep the foot cupped in your hand so it cannot puncture the uterus as you manipulate.

If you need to repel (i.e. push back inside) a head or limb to get the bit you need into the right place, it is useful to put a sterile tape or lambing rope onto it so that you can both find and identify it again. If you place a head rope, it is OK to use a slip loop as long as you locate

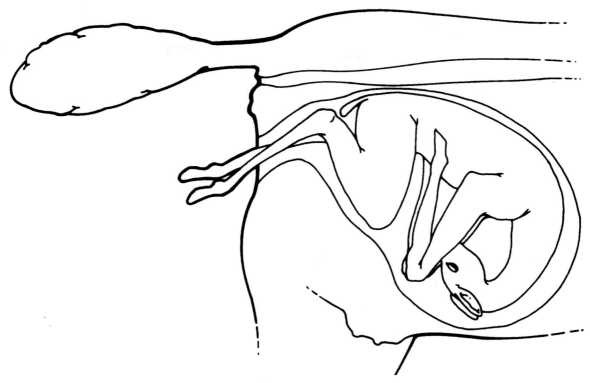

'Normal' breech presentation. Breech births are relatively rare. If the feet are presented as in this drawing, they are deliverable. More commonly the feet will be forward, and will require manipulation to bring them into the birth canal ahead of the rump of the cria.

it so that the V of the gap in it will pull straight (*see* photographs opposite). If you line it up like that it won't tighten.

Posterior Presentations

With this presentation, the cria is back to front. You won't be able to turn these around and deliver them front first: they have to come out back feet first. Therefore you are aiming to have both the back feet straight in the birth canal, with the baby the right way up (i.e. its feet pointing the same way as the mother's feet – *see* illustration above).

Manipulation of hind legs is more awkward, and you must take great care not to puncture the uterus with a hock or hoof. You will need to repel the rump of the cria back into the mother to give yourself sufficient room for this.

The worry with breech births is that when the cord comes through the birth canal, and gets pinched, it stops the blood supply to the baby and stimulates it to start breathing, so you have very little time to get its head into the air so it won't suffocate. But you still have to be gentle! Better to lose the cria than to lose the mother by injuring her. A true breech presentation, where only the tail is presented and the feet are forward, will almost certainly require a vet to correct it.

Exhaustion

You can help deliver a correctly presented baby if the mother is too tired (often the case if you have needed to correct a malpresentation). Don't pull too hard! Work with the mother's contractions and just lean a bit of extra weight behind them. Tissues stretch gradually, so using the same pressure for fifteen to twenty seconds will help, even though at first you don't seem to be getting anywhere. Don't tug! Lean, gradually. The best place to hold a leg is the cannon bone, i.e. the lower long bone of the front leg, below the knee. You may need gently to ease the birth canal wall backwards over the head with a flat, lubricated hand. Pull slightly downwards, i.e. towards the mother's hocks. If the limb is very slippery you can improve grip with a piece of absolutely clean paper towel between your hand and the leg. Soft nylon lambing cords or tapes can be used if you have them sterilized ready, and should be looped in a slip loop above the fetlock. You will usually find most resistance as the chest/shoulders are delivered, and it is worth rotating the baby to an angle of about 45 degrees and pulling one leg at a time to make best use of the widest part of the birth canal. Do be gentle! Too much force can bruise the baby's lungs, and lacerate the birth canal.

If you have followed the above guidelines you should be making visible progress by the time you've been pulling about five minutes. If you aren't, stop. You need expert help.

Other Complications

If you can see the mother pushing but nothing is showing even after thirty to sixty minutes

---

Case History

A cria that presented forward (i.e. head first) but with bent knees (i.e. carpal flexion) was successfully delivered despite the fact that it was not possible to straighten the knees. These straightened as they were delivered and the cria and mother were fine.

(Martyn Jose, personal communication.)

---

or so of lusty effort, you need to have a look to see what is wrong. If, when you gently advance your clean, gloved, lubricated hand up top side of the birth canal, you run into a tight band of tough-feeling tissue, you have probably either got a twisted uterus or a ring womb (undilated cervix) and you need a vet. However, if you can feel the baby, you need to figure out which bit is being presented before you can know how to help. If it's a breech, you should be able to feel the tail and bottom. The middle joint of the hind leg bends the opposite way to the bottom joint. With front legs, the knee and fetlock (middle and bottom) joints bend the same way, and you have the useful clue of a head and neck near where the legs meet the body. Make sure that the two legs you are trying to guide into the birth canal come from the same end of the same baby!

CHAPTER 12

Care of the Newborn

THE FIRST HOURS

After the birth, the female does not lick her baby. She will remain close to it, hum, and sniff it, touching noses. Often she will also make a soft clucking noise. If approached, she will be very solicitous and concerned for the cria, but will not attempt physical contact with it. The white, gummy, epidermal membrane, which covers the new baby rather like cling film (most clearly visible in the photographs on page 166), is a normal feature of camelid newborns, and some theorize that it provides wind protection while the fleece dries, so that licking it off would be counter productive, and harm the survival chances of the baby.

The cria will usually begin to attempt to get to its feet within an hour, and should achieve this considerable accomplishment within two hours. It will then start seeking the udder and learning how to feed. The mother should remain close, waiting patiently while it wobbles and nudges, trying to figure out what to do. If disturbed, the mother may respond to the cria's attempts to stand by moving away, presumably in an attempt to encourage it to follow her away from a threat. The behaviour of the mother may range from the alarm and confusion sometimes seen with maiden animals, to aggression and spitting towards any approach, but most often they become unusually tame to handle, and will follow if the cria is picked up and carried to another location.

SUCKLING

The mother will stand still when the cria attempts to feed, and it quickly learns to suck at all four of the teats in turn. It will feed often throughout the day, two or three times per hour in daylight, at first. It feeds only for a short period (often less than a minute) at each time. Over the course of twenty-four hours, the cria will take about 10 per cent of its bodyweight in milk. The best guide to the success of suckling is the energy displayed by the cria; within a day or two of birth it should be starting to expend extra energy in play. It is normal for the cria to lose half a kilo (a pound) or so in bodyweight in the first few days before it begins to gain weight.

Colostrum

The first milk secreted by the mammary gland after birth (in all mammals) is termed colostrum. It is rich in immune proteins, called immunoglobulins, or antibodies, which are absorbed by the newborn animal and then circulate in the bloodstream. There they provide protection from early infection while the youngster's own immune system develops sufficiently to manage on its own. Because the newborn animal's body takes no active part in the immunity it receives in this way from its mother, it is called Passive Immunity. When born, llama and alpaca crias have no immunoglobulin G (IgG) in their bloodstream, but after drinking their first few meals of colostrum, levels in both llamas and alpacas

Suckling. Note that the cria's tail is down, indicating that it has found the teat and is drinking. (Photo: Karen Oglesby, Meon Valley Alpacas)

should rise to 2,500mg/dl. Blood testing can measure the level, and provide an indication of the success of the transfer of passive immunity via colostrum. The level should remain high for the first ten days of life, after which it gradually declines to about 1,500mg/dl over the second ten days.

Colostrum contains other elements absent from normal milk, too. These include a higher level of fat, less lactose and more Vitamins and minerals than normal milk. There are also white blood cells and a substance called complement, which help to protect the newborn gut from infectious organisms.

Closure

During the first hours of life, the newborn mammal's gut is specially adapted to absorb the large immune protein molecules from colostrum unchanged, without digesting them and breaking them down. Once several milk meals have been consumed, a change occurs making this absorption impossible. The stomach in the newly born animal has no acid to help break down proteins, but within a few hours of birth, acid secretion begins, and with it, protein breakdown. It is therefore very important that the newborn receives colostrum, rather than ordinary milk, because the gut will close to immune proteins whether or not any are absorbed. If this window is missed, it becomes impossible for the new cria to get its immune protein by drinking it.

ESSENTIAL SIGNS AND INDICATORS

Newborn llamas and alpacas have the same potential problems to overcome as other newborn animals, assuming normal health when born. These are chilling, predators, and infection. In addition, they depend upon getting good nourishment and maternal care.

There are a number of signs and indicators that will help you to assess the health and wellbeing of the newborn cria.

First Feed

One of the most obvious indicators is the speed with which the cria rises to feed. These animals have evolved to survive in the harsh environment of the altiplano, a high-altitude, arid place, which is very cold at night. This explains why they are almost always born early in the day: if they were born near to sunset, they would die of exposure before having a chance to get to their feet and feed.

A cria that is not rising to feed within an hour or two of birth has a problem.

Weight

The normal birth weight for alpaca crias varies between 3.6–10.4kg (8–23lb); llama crias are about twice as big, between 8 and 20kg (18 and 45lb). It is usual for them to lose half a kilo (1lb) or so in the first few days of life, but a greater degree of weight loss than

The objective: the cria is up, safe, and feeding happily from its attentive, solicitous mother.
(Photo: Chris Eke, UK Llamas)

that should signal a problem to you. A spring balance is the simplest device to check birth and subsequent weights, as long as you have a convenient hook from which to hang it. An old holdall, or any large soft bag, is suitable to suspend the cria in to be weighed.

Once weight gain starts, llama crias initially about 250g (½lb) daily rising to 500g (1lb) a day after about two weeks. With alpaca crias these corresponding gains are about half of those of llamas.

Temperature
The normal body temperature of the newly born cria is 37.7–38.9ºC (100–102ºF), the same as the mother's, but once it has adjusted to the ambient temperature, this can be a bit less stable and may rise to 39.2ºC (102.5ºF) without signalling any disease.

Heart Rate
Heart rates should be sixty to ninety beats per minute, and breathing rate ten to thirty breaths per minute. Llamas and alpacas have to breathe through their noses, so mouth breathing indicates distress, and obstruction of the nasal airways is a serious problem for them.

Behaviour
Thriving crias play. Within days of birth young crias will be spending significant portions of each day chasing each other about. Play is a sensitive indicator of health. If a youngster is not joining in, then it has a problem: time to investigate.

CHILLING

Although the altiplano is cold and windy, it is not wet, and cold rain on the back of a newborn cria can easily chill it sufficiently to kill it. Long dewy or frosty grass can soak a cria that is struggling to gain its feet as effectively as rain. It is speculated that the epidermal membrane in which crias are born forms a windproof layer over the fleece to give it a sort of wetsuit for protection from wind-chill. This protection cannot work if the membrane does not dry. The mechanism to maintain

One youngster urges another to forsake his sunbathing for a game. (Photo: Peter Watson, South West Alpacas)

Alpaca crias spend quite a lot of time playing; indeed, play is a sensitive indicator of health, and individuals who do not join in usually have a problem of some kind. (Photo: Karen Oglesby, Meon Valley Alpacas)

body temperature does not function so well in premature animals, and their body temperature must be monitored carefully.

If you wish to minimize losses owed to weather, you must have a building into which the mother and baby can go until the weather improves and/or the cria is strong enough to withstand a soaking. Since it is distressing for the female to be away from her group, her shelter needs to be either within sight of them, or large enough to accommodate both her and a companion animal as well.

To Dry or Not to Dry

Because of the epidermal membrane and its theoretical use, some breeders feel that they should refrain from removing it by drying a weak or cold cria. In my experience, despite the fact that llama and alpaca females never lick their young (nature's equivalent of a good towelling), drying and massaging a newborn cria definitely seems to help to warm, stimulate and invigorate it. My justification for 'going against nature' in this way is that nature is wasteful, and uses death to select for stronger, more vigorous individuals. Most breeders would rather save animals where possible, and have a larger number from which to select animals on other grounds. The high potential value of the newborn llama and alpaca mean that few of us are content to leave the weak but saveable cria to the dubious mercy of nature.

A stock of clean old towels, therefore, is a handy resource, as are other weather defences, such cria coats, survival blankets, and fleece pet beds to lift the cria up from the cold ground. These aids should all be laundered between uses.

Old, clean towels and a thermometer. Low-tech equipment can still be absolutely vital in caring for newborn animals.

This late-born cria has a specially designed coat to help keep it warm and dry. In poor weather, such measures can make the difference between life and death for a newborn cria. (Photo: Jean Field, Devon Alpacas)

PREDATORS

Predation of newborn crias is not a big problem in the UK. However, predators are by their very nature opportunist, and there is no reason to suppose that foxes, badgers, crows or dogs would not attack newborn crias if given the chance, especially if they are short of other sources of food. I have a personal report of a cria dying quickly in an attack by a flock of crows during harsh weather. Since you will not normally have stud males (who might chase off predators) in calving paddocks, it is important to have your calving areas situated where they are easy to observe and to protect. Dogs could be a particular problem because many of them are larger than wild predators, and there are records of dog attacks on fully grown llamas and alpacas in the UK, so one cannot assume that they would be chased away by the adults in the group.

GETTING NOURISHMENT

This is perhaps the greatest cause of concern for breeders of llamas and alpacas. You have your (apparently) normal healthy cria on the ground, but will it rise and feed, and will its mother let it? The hurdles it has to overcome are in part already discussed – in chilling and predation, but physical capability and co-operation of the mother, as well as her ability to provide milk, are just as crucial.

It is useful to have to hand a bottle, teat, stomach tube and frozen colostrum or

Early attempts to locate the nipple can be some way off the mark, but the raised tail, and jerky, pushy muzzle movements show what she has in mind. (Photo: Dick Hobbs)

The raised tail of this cria shows that she is still looking for the nipple. A lowering of the tail will indicate that she has found the nipple and is feeding successfully. (Photo: Jean Field, Devon Alpacas)

colostrum substitute. Frozen plasma (*see* opposite) is excellent if you can arrange it.

Failure of Passive Immunity (FPI)

This is a term used when the cria (or calf or lamb etc) does not receive sufficient colostrum to give it good blood levels of antibody. It will be more subject to infections, and often fail to grow and thrive. It is possible for your vet to do blood tests on newborn crias to determine whether they have sufficient immunoglobulins. These tests should definitely be performed in crias where there is reason to believe they may not have had a good feed of high-quality colostrum, especially if the animal is of high value.

Colostrum Supplements

The colostrum from another species of animal also kept on the same farm will provide some protection. The most suitable is that of goats, which most nearly matches the composition of camelid colostrum. It is important to keep only the 'first drawn' colostrum, though, because this has a much higher concentration of antibodies than that of the second and subsequent days, even though the udder produces something recognizable as colostrum for three or four days. It is important that the donor for the colostrum is disease free (for example, from Johne's disease) and vaccinated against the same diseases as the llamas or alpacas. Cow colostrum is also suitable; that of sheep is probably a bit too high in fat.

The new cria needs about 10 per cent of its bodyweight in colostrum during the first twenty-four hours of life. The very first feed will only be about a tenth of this, and two-hourly feeding is recommended so that the capacity of the stomach is not exceeded.

Plasma Treatment for FPI

If a cria has not enough immunoglobulin, it can be transfused with plasma from a healthy adult animal. Ideally this donor animal should come from the same farm, so that it will have immunity from the kinds of infection the new cria is likely to face. Plasma can be stored frozen, so it may be harvested in advance and kept in case of need. The donor animal does not need to be the mother of the cria, and fully grown (gelded or entire) males make good donors, since they have little drain on their own physiology. Blood is collected from the donor animal and then taken to a special (large) centrifuge to have the cells removed, after which it can be frozen and stored for up to two years.

Reasons for FPI

Reasons for FPI include crias that are premature or weak and failure of the mother to allow feeding.

Weak/Premature Crias

If a cria is premature, it may be too feeble to rise and seek the udder. It will require help and possibly even supplementary feeding until it gains enough strength to manage alone. Many newborn crias have a low blood sugar when they are born, and with premature ones this can compromise their ability to get to their feet and feed. Premature crias can be identified by their uncut incisor teeth, still enveloped in gum, by the adherent soft pads on their feet (with mature-term crias these drop off in six to twelve hours), and by floppy ears. Occasionally they will have soft tendons, so that when they do stand, or are supported in a weight-bearing position, the fetlocks reach the ground. They often pant in a distressed way immediately after birth, although this can be observed in full-term crias too. In other species, prematurity affects the efficiency with which the lungs exchange oxygen, and we assume that this is the same with llamas and alpacas. This would contribute to weakness and difficulty in gaining their feet to feed.

Failure of the Mother to Allow Feeding

Some females are not patient enough to allow the cria to find the udder. They may well wander off, and if there is a group of females

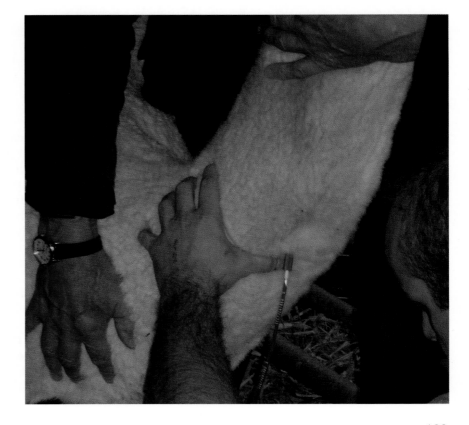

Collection of blood from a healthy adult animal. This is not a painful or distressing process for the donor. (Photo: Tom Chamberlain)

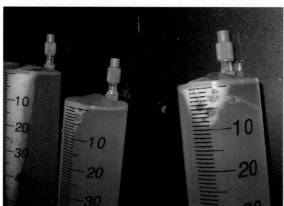

Capped 50ml syringes of plasma ready for immediate use or for freezing. When thawing frozen syringes, do not microwave them: that destroys the immune proteins. (Photo: Tom Chamberlain)

in the field, the cria can become confused. The best solution to this problem seems to be to place the new mother and her baby alone together in a small pen – but in sight of the group. Usually, if left together for the rest of the day and the night, they will have figured out who is who and have bonded by the morning. Some mothers are restless and will not allow the cria to feed until they have passed the placenta. (This is also called the afterbirth, or the 'cleansing'. The process of passing it is also called cleansing.) Usually llama and alpaca mothers are very good and attentive, but it is likely that the longer we breed them away from the harsh environments of South America, the less mothering ability will come into the selection criteria, and this situation will become increasingly common.

No Milk (Agalactia)

The mother may fail to produce enough, or any milk. This is one of the most difficult situations to judge. The action of sucking the udder stimulates milk let down, so simply supplementing the cria with replacement colostrum is not the ideal answer, since you would like ultimately for the mother to establish a milk supply and to do the job herself. Usually, in time, the mother will start to produce milk, and the cria needs to be encouraged to keep trying to find it. Sometimes an injection of oxytocin can help with milk let down, and this can be repeated every four to six hours. Warm water bathing and massaging of the udder may help stimulate oxytocin secretion, too. If the cria is a bit premature, it seems that the mammary gland is not ready for lactation. In the meantime, the cria must be supplemented sufficiently (with colostrum in the first twenty-four to forty-eight hours) to keep its strength up. If lactation fails totally, it will require hand-rearing.

Mastitis

This is an inflammation of the mammary gland, which may make the mother ill, and incidentally cause failure of milk production. The udder (or part of it, since mastitis can affect only one quarter) will typically be firm, hot and swollen. You may notice the mother looking or behaving ill, walking awkwardly, or the cria looking tucked up and miserable. When mastitis is suspected, the vet should be called without delay to ensure that treatment is started as early as possible, otherwise permanent damage to the gland could result. Although nursing usually need not be prevented (the stomach acid should kill bacteria) a mastitic udder may well not produce enough (or any) milk.

HAND-REARING

This is the only option with crias whose mothers die, fail to produce milk, or reject them (this last is fairly rare). There is a number of suitable milk replacers available; goat or sheep milk replacers work pretty well. Calf milk replacer is not recommended because cow milk has too high a level of lactose and this would be expected to upset the digestion of camelids, whose own milk has high levels of fat and protein, but relatively low ones of lactose.

Some orphaned crias can become adept at stealing milk from other mothers who are feeding their own cria. The success of this strategy depends upon the cria's cunning and also a degree of acquiescence by the other females, but it can contribute significantly to the orphaned cria's nutrition.

Bottle-Feeding

Most crias will not learn to drink from a bucket, and some will have difficulty adjusting to a mixture of bottle and natural feeding, preferring one or the other.

The bottle should be held level, to reduce the risk of choking. For newborn animals use a teat with a tiny hole, so that not too much milk is delivered for it to swallow without choking. As it gains strength the hole can be made bigger by cutting a cross through it.

Stomach-Tubing

It may be necessary when handrearing a cria to stomach-tube it to supply milk, if it is reluctant to feed from a bottle, or more likely, it is receiving some nourishment from its mother, but not enough. In that instance bottle feeding can be problematic, with the mother objecting to the cria coming to feed, and leading it away. The only way to manage the situation is often to catch and restrain the cria and use a stomach tube A restrained cria will rarely suck voluntarily on a teat, but will often resist stomach tubing only minimally.

The stomach tube should have an outside diameter no wider than 10–13mm (up to half an inch) and should be open at the end, not the side. It should be passed via the mouth, and the head should be kept semi-flexed so that it does not pass into the windpipe. The tube should be wetted with water to help it slide up the mouth to the throat and gently advanced as the cria makes a swallowing movement. You should be able to feel it going down the left side of the neck in the oesophagus. If it is in the windpipe, you cannot feel the tube because of the cartilage rings in the trachea. Push it as far as the point where the neck joins the chest. It should not be pushed as far as the stomach, because that will cause the milk to be deposited in the wrong stomach compartment (C1): if liquid milk passes through the chest portion of the oesophagus, it may well help to trigger the reflex that causes it to be passed directly into the correct part of the stomach (C3). This is important for two reasons. The first is that if the milk ends up in C1, it cannot be absorbed from its lining. The second is that milk in C1 can be fermented and produce toxic substances, making the cria ill.

It is a good idea to have cord attached to the mouth end of the tube so that you can retain hold of it if the cria struggles and swallows: It has been known for the tube to disappear inside the cria never to emerge! One difficulty is that a lamb stomach tube (which is the type easily available), is a bit short for the long neck of a cria, so the mouth end is usually quite close to the exit of the mouth. That means that it is relatively easy to lose hold of it.

Milking Camelids

This is extremely difficult because camelid teats are small and not pendulous, so they are difficult to get hold of even if your female is quiet enough to let you try. Camelid colostrum is low volume, and inclined to solidify on contact with air, so it is difficult to feed back to the cria as well.

It is possible to make a hand pump to help with drawing off milk, using a syringe. This should be a 20ml plastic syringe, with a rubber plunger. The end onto which the needle normally fits is cut off, leaving an open tube, and the plunger removed and reversed. Thus the plunger is inserted into the 'wrong' end of the syringe barrel, and the flanged end used to fit over the teat. Then suction is applied using the plunger, and milk harvested into the syringe. It is a fiddly and difficult job, but milking by hand is virtually impossible.

PHYSICAL HAZARDS

In addition to a suitable building where a new or weak cria can be protected from the weather, the paddocks used for females and their new babies should be properly fenced and free of hazards into which a youngster may stumble. This is an important consideration since fencing does not need to be particularly good to keep adult animals in; a new cria may simply walk under or through it. Ditches, banks and ponds are likewise a hazard for the unwary. If your land possesses these, at least ensure that they are checked several times a day so that a wayward baby can be rescued.

INFECTIONS

The Navel

The navel is potentially an excellent place for bacteria to grow, and is at risk from colonization by the bugs which normally inhabit the environment around the newly born cria.

Routine disinfection of the navel in the newly born cria is usual. This has been carried out with a variety of disinfectants, often iodine based. For swiftness and convenience, many breeders use Terramycin antibiotic spray. This is stained blue so it is easy to see whether it has been done, and contains the broad-spectrum antibiotic oxytetracycline. The theoretical drawback with this treatment is that you may eventually select for bacteria that are resistant to oxytetracycline, and the spray will become ineffective. However, because use of the spray should be limited (i.e. only on navels or occasional open wounds), the chance of this occurring should remain quite small.

Murray Fowler (*see* Further Reading and Bibliography) recommends the use of chlorhexidine in a preparation called Nolvasan. This is a disinfectant, rather than an antibiotic, so it should pose fewer problems of resistance, and its use has been demonstrated to reduce bacterial counts on the navels of newly born foals. It performed much better than the iodine-based disinfectants tested in the same trial.

Specific Infections

To avoid problems in the young crias of Clostridial infection or Coccidial infestation, the areas used for calving should be rotated and not overused. Infective levels of these pathogens can build up on the ground with successive use, and later crias can be exposed to very high levels of infection, which will overwhelm any resistance they may have or get from colostrum. The typical scenario with 'dirty' calving areas is that of crias that are apparently healthy when born, but then become ill instead of thriving and growing.

As the crias start to take grass (they will start to nibble at it from about two weeks of age, although significant amounts are not eaten at this stage), they become exposed to parasitic worm eggs. Young animals are most susceptible to these infestations, so a prevention programme is essential.

Clostridial Diseases

These are caused by a family of bacteria called *Clostridia*. They are frequently fatal and include tetanus, severe enteritis (characterized by severe diarrhoea) and gangrene-type conditions. In other species where these diseases are also a problem, vaccines have been developed to protect against them, and these vaccines have been used in camelids. Unfortunately, since they are not licensed in llamas and alpacas, there has been no requirement to test them in these animals, and therefore we have no idea whether they really work. The picture is further confused by the fact that the diseases tend to be sporadic and they aren't really transmitted directly between animals (usually they are contracted from a common source in the environment). The result is that an unvaccinated herd might naturally go for years without an outbreak, while, because the vaccines do not work against every possible strain (even if the vaccine does work in camelids) a vaccinated herd might get a case.

Overhandling

Llama and alpaca crias are dangerously appealing and cute. There is a great human tendency to wish to pet and cuddle, and the additional pathos of an orphaned cria's situation frequently adds to this desire. However, over handling and familiarization by humans of infant camelids has disastrous consequences, producing an adult which fails to appreciate that humans are a distinct species from its own. The result of this so called 'imprinting' is a llama or alpaca which treats humans like one of its own species. Since humans are small and weak, the imprinted animal expects to dominate and take precedence over them. Over familiarized animals typically barge, spit, bite and kick humans. Some will rear and knock people off their feet, and then kneel on them to injure them further. These are all methods of attack they use with their own species, underlining their failure to perceive humans as different.

Once an animal has been habituated to human contact in this way, it frequently becomes impossible and even dangerous to handle, and must be destroyed, making all the effort of hand-rearing it futile.

Vaccination

Llamas and alpacas tend to have a high individual worth, either in monetary terms or in sentimental value to their owners – frequently both. For that reason, and the fact that vaccines appear to do little harm in almost all cases, most owners elect to vaccinate. Vaccines change from time to time, and opinions on the best one to use and the best way to use it also change on a fairly frequent basis. The best thing to do is to discuss vaccination regimes with your vet, who may be, or wish to become, a member of the British Veterinary Camelid Society. The BVCS keeps up with current thinking and events in the camelid veterinary world, and provides your vet with a means to determine current best practice.

CHAPTER 13

Common Health Problems

When animals are domesticated, they are almost inevitably kept at higher population densities and in different habitats than they would be if wild. Many – if not all – of the health problems they suffer are as a consequence of these two factors. This is why it can be said, 'Health is Husbandry, Husbandry is Health.'

Llamas and alpacas are domesticated from animals evolved to live at low population densities in a poor environment, where large distances have to be covered to find sufficient food. The forage itself is tough, deep rooted and fairly low in energy value. Temperatures are fairly extreme in daily range, sunlight levels are high, but rainfall is low. It is not really surprising, therefore, that when we pack them in at four or five to the acre on lush, soft grasses in small paddocks, with winter day-length down to eight hours and high levels of rainfall, that we get a few problems. It is more surprising that we don't get more but, overall, llamas and alpacas are a hardy and healthy bunch.

This chapter is not designed to be used as a substitute for advice from your vet. A sick animal should always be examined and treated professionally. Rather it is to help you keep

Familiarity with your animals as individuals gives you enormous advantages in managing their health and in detecting disease.

Medicines

There are no drugs licensed for camelids, so all drug treatment is given on a 'best guess' basis, and doses are similarly guesswork.

your animals in such a way that the risks of common health problems are minimized and to help you recognize problems before they become serious. The weird and the wonderful will catch us all out.

DIGESTIVE PROBLEMS

Teeth

Mastication is the first stage of the digestion process, so problems with the teeth can be expected to affect nutrition. The teeth are designed to do lots of work, and problems with them are relatively frequent. The incisors often grow beyond the dental pad, either because of congenital abnormalities or the softness of UK forages (or both) and are very commonly trimmed at shearing. (Dentition and information on trimming are described in Chapter 5.) A more serious problem is when there is a short lower jaw and the teeth fail to reach the dental pad. This makes them wear on the hard palate, often damaging it and dramatically reducing the efficiency with which they can cut off long forage.

Tooth Abscesses

The most common tooth problem noticed by owners is a persistent swelling in the face, usually, but not always, in the lower jaw. On investigation, this may be hard or soft, depending on whether bony tissue is involved, but generally it persists and enlarges over time, because it is almost always an abscess. Usually this starts by being centred around a tooth, but can, if untreated, track into the jawbone and even into the soft tissues of the head and neck. Other symptoms of tooth problems can be loss of weight, reluctance to feed, feed dropping out of the mouth, and foul-smelling breath. Abscesses do not usually discharge to the outside, although they can do, especially when apparently caused by a failure of eruption of permanent teeth (observed in two cases to my own knowledge). Any of these symptoms, if they persist, should be investigated by your vet.

Treatment of tooth and jaw abscesses is difficult, because once the infection gets into the bone it can be very hard to shift. The best success is seen with the removal of the affected tooth and any infected bone associated with it under anaesthetic, plus antibiotics, but repeated operations can be necessary to eradicate infection. Expect a big bill and an uncertain outcome. Use of a relatively new antibiotic, florfenicol (trade name Nuflor) has been associated with a successful outcome when used early on in the disease.

The best you can do to help prevent tooth and jaw abscesses is to reduce what are called 'risk factors'. These include:

- Spiky hay and forage.
  Hay made from cereal crops is not common in the UK but has been associated with increased incidence in America. Some plants have hard, barbed seeds, which tend to get into the gums and track down beside the teeth, taking infection down with them and starting the abscess off. It has been noted that Peruvian grass is extremely spiky, and it has been speculated that grazed forage

may be less of a risk than that fed as hay. Having said that, jaw abscesses are well recognized in South America; they almost always result in casualty slaughter of the animal because treatment is uneconomic.

- Overgrown incisor crowns.
  David Anderson from Ohio thinks that excessively long incisors force the animal to realign its jaw to allow a proper bite. This alteration in the jaw apposition produces a mismatch between the molars, and this predisposes them to problems with their roots. Trimming is therefore necessary. However, overzealous trimming can damage the pulp and cause disease by letting infection in. It is recommended that fighting teeth should have a 2mm crown left behind, to avoid cutting into the pulp cavity.

- Routinely rasping molar teeth.
  This procedure should be reserved for animals with specific identified problems, and not carried out as a routine, because it removes the normal sharp cutting edge of the tooth and reduces its grinding effectiveness. Sharp points on the edges of the wearing surfaces of molars are a normal feature of llama and alpaca mouths, and rarely seem to cause laceration of cheeks or tongue.

Face Abscesses

Very occasionally a face abscess can arise in soft tissue, not involving the jaw bone. Sometimes the parotid salivary gland is involved, but in any event these non-bone abscesses have a much better prognosis.

Other possible causes of jaw swellings are tumours, bone cysts, salivary cysts and stings or bites: your vet is the best person to sort out what is going on.

Choke

In this condition the animal swallows inadequately chewed food, which then lodges in the oesophagus (gullet) and fails to pass into the stomach, causing a blockage.

This can occur especially if greedy or dominant animals are competing over titbits like apples, and fatal choke involving an apple

Long-term overstocking of animals and reliance on concentrate feeds is likely to lead to stress, digestive disturbance, and ulceration of the stomach.

lodged in the oesophagus, which it was not possible to remove, has been seen. Ensure that such keenly sought foods are shaped in long thin pieces, which will not get stuck. Signs of choke are drooling, obvious distress and discomfort, and failure to eat or drink.

Colic

Colic is a clinical sign, not a diagnosis. All it means is abdominal pain. As such, it can have a variety of causes, because anything that causes inflammation (for example, an abscess in the abdomen) or obstruction to the passage of food and fluid through the digestive system, may result in pain. Even pneumonia, by inflaming the lining of the chest, can cause signs of abdominal pain. Other possible causes are liver disease, inflammation of the pancreas, peritonitis, twisted gut, uterine torsion and kidney or bladder problems. Bloat, the accumulation of gas in C1, is rare.

The colicky animal will behave abnormally. It will stop chewing the cud. It may adopt a strange posture, appear restless, lie down (but don't forget that they bask in the sun and roll as part of their normal behaviour) and shift about. They may get up and down often and, if down, keep shifting from lying on their sides to lying on their chests, or lie on their chests with their back legs stretched

out to the side. Sometimes they will exhibit these signs for twenty minutes or so and then stop, having recovered.

It is rare for alpacas and llamas with colic to throw themselves about with the violence of a colicky horse, and very often the fairly subtle signs of abdominal pain are soon suppressed by the development of the dullness of dehydration and shock, and all you see is a recumbent animal that is obviously sick. If you handle the animal, it may be clear to you that it does not want its abdomen touched. Because of the variety of different possible causes of colic, persistent signs of abdominal discomfort warrant a call to the vet.

Constipation

There are several conditions that can cause an animal to strain as if trying to defecate or urinate (also known as tenesmus). True constipation is an obstruction or increased resistance to the passage of faeces through the bowel, and because urinary blockage is more rapidly fatal than true constipation it should first be eliminated as a possible cause of straining, as should dystocia (obstructed birth).

Impaction of the large bowel (usually the spiral colon) with tangled accumulations of fibrous plant food, or coat fibre, have been recognized. In mild cases a drench of liquid paraffin may help but, if the blockage is complete, the bowel will often respond to it by stopping its peristaltic movements. When that happens, there is no way for the liquid paraffin to reach the obstruction, and surgery is the only way to save the animal. Signs of colic may be seen.

Plant Poisoning

Alpacas kept on a weedy, mixed sward have on occasion become ill, appearing poisoned, exhibiting malaise, frothing at the mouth, and collapse. Apparent recovery has been followed by regurgitation of gut contents. Six animals in a group became affected in a similar way. There was obvious pain. The animals were treated symptomatically with Effadryl (a rehydration salt-mix drench) and eventually recovered. The culprit toxin was never identified, so very rough grazing carries a general warning: camelids appear to have little natural skill at determining which plants will be toxic. Eric Hoffman has proposed that this is a result of evolution in a protected alpine environment where such plant species are not encountered. It is likely that all of the plants our animals consume in the UK are absent from their natural range, so to eat anything at all here is a matter of experimentation for them. Accordingly, do not suppose that they will know better than to consume a toxic plant if it is offered to them. It is more likely that at least one of a group will try it and, if it is palatable to that individual, they all will.

Alpacas and llamas love blackberries and may well try any other berry in the hope that it will be similar.

There have been reports of toxicity from elder, daisies and hawthorn. Buttercups are a known irritant. Rhododendron poisoning produces attempts to vomit. It has been successfully treated with kaolin (Kaogel) drench. Since rhododendron poisoning is normally fatal, this or perhaps another adsorbent, such as bismuth and charcoal, may be worth trying as a treatment as early as possible.

It would be expected that grazing of quantities of bracken or oak would be poisonous.

Oak poisoning has been recorded only in young crias eating a large quantity of oak leaves, although adult animals have been seen to eat what has seemed like a lot of acorns with no apparent ill effects. Similarly, ragwort is highly poisonous in other species, and it may appear in hay, especially if made from a weedy sward. Usually ragwort in its green form is found to be unpalatable by stock, including alpacas and llamas, but once dried it will be eaten readily. The toxins are still present in the dried plant and poisoning will result if it is eaten in hay.

Diseases of the Digestive Tract

The first two stomach chambers, which digest fibre, rely on a stable chemical environment to work properly. (*See* Chapter 4). Animals that are fed too much concentrate feed may well suffer disturbances in the delicate balance of bacteria, which is essential to the process of digestion. This may in turn place them at a disadvantage in coping with stress.

Ulcers

Ulcers are fairly commonly identified in sick animals, and it is not really clear whether they are a primary cause of illness or a symptom of it. Too much acidity and too little protection of the stomach lining by mucus seem to be associated with gastric ulceration in other species. We do know that inappropriate feeding, especially too high a level of concentrates and too little fibre, plus chronic (i.e. long-term) stress are associated with stomach ulcers in true ruminants. Overstocking has been seen associated with an outbreak of ulcers, where there was a heavy reliance on concentrate feeding because of lack of pasture. It is possible that overcrowding will also lead to extra stress on the animals, predisposing them further to ulceration.

Ulcers or wrong feeding will not produce evidence in dung samples. We do not yet have any tests that will give us this information. Occult (hidden digested) blood is not seen in ulcer cases in llamas and alpacas, even though it is in other species.

Ulceration is hard to diagnose in the living animal. There are some non-specific hints of it in certain blood tests. Ulceration appears to occur rarely in animals fed a diet of grass, hay, alfalfa and Camelibra.

There have been reports of ulcer cases being cured by treatment with omeprazole (an antacid drug) and antepsin, and these drugs have been recommended by vets in Australia. Gastroguard is a horse preparation containing omeprazole, and could be used in advance of predicted stress to try to protect the stomach from ulceration.

Liver Conditions

One of the significant ailments to affect the liver is hepatic adiposity/lipidosis, in which too much fat is laid down in the liver. It is caused by incorrect diet, and can be devastating. It is seen in zoo llamas, and causes a decrease in liver function. It has been seen in an apparently otherwise healthy youngster, and five cases in one unit occurred where part of the cause was an overstocking/overfeeding problem.

Other conditions of the liver include stunted livers: small livers (only 1.5kg/3lb in weight) have been seen incidentally at post-mortem. Heart disease can cause secondary liver failure. Scarring of the liver, from previous parasite infestation with the worm *Lamanema,* can be seen in imported animals. (The parasite itself seems invariably to be eradicated during quarantine.) Liver cancer has occasionally been a cause of sudden death.

Johne's Disease

This disease affects the large and small intestines, causing weakness and diarrhoea. It is caused by a bacterium that is related to TB. Alpacas have been reported to get it, but some seem able to self-cure, without becoming chronic carriers. Feeding of colostrum from an infected animal to a cria (for example if cow or goat colostrum from infected animals were used) is a route by which they may catch it.

NUTRITION

Problems can arise as a result of either excess nutrition or a nutritional deficiency. The condition most commonly caused by an excess is obesity. This can in turn lead to a range of other problems including infertility and liver and digestive problems.

Deficiencies arise when there is a lack of certain nutrients in the diet. Deficiences in Vitamin D, selenium, copper, cobalt, zinc and magnesium can all lead either to specific conditions (listed under the body system primarily affected) or to a general lack of resistance to other disease. *See* Chapter 3 for strategies to prevent the development of deficiency disease.

Skeletal Problems

Vitamin D Deficiency (Rickets)

Rickets is the major problem seen in these latitudes: Vitamin D is normally manufactured under the skin in a process dependent upon sunlight, and the short winter days and gloomy skies mean that this does not happen sufficiently well. Angular limb deformities are often seen (i.e. the young animals grow with bent legs, commonly knock knees on the front), but occasionally a youngster is so badly affected that it moves stiffly and reluctantly, lying about instead of playing with its mates. Stiffness, lameness and weight loss (probably due to failure to feed adequately) have been seen in older, pregnant animals, too. Blood samples may show raised phosphorus levels.

Many experienced breeders recommend treatment with injectable Vitamin D at two-monthly intervals throughout the winter to counter this problem. The preparation most often used is a combined treatment with vitamins ADE. The vitamins A and E seem to do no harm.

Selenium Deficiency (White Muscle Disease)

Selenium is a trace element that is either plentiful or deficient depending on local geology. Deficiency can cause a range of problems including unthriftiness and infertility in both

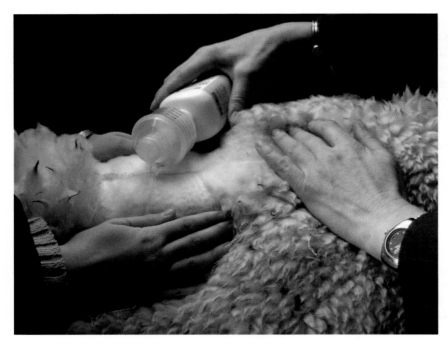

Correct application of a pour-on worm medicine, such as Eprinex or Dectomax. The fleece must be parted along the topline so that the product is delivered to the skin – it must be absorbed through the skin in order to work. Any medicine that runs out through the fleece is wasted.

the male and female, poor resistance to infection, and muscle damage and weakness. Herbage should be analysed to determine mineral content and it should be supplemented if in low levels. It is worth remembering that a relative abundance of other elements such as silver, arsenic, cadmium, copper, mercury, lead, zinc and sulphur can all interfere with selenium uptake and cause a relative deficiency.

PARASITES

Worms

The classic sign that your animals have worms is diarrhoea, but they can also become quite suddenly ill and poor without showing diarrhoea. Diarrhoea takes time to develop, and in a massive acute infestation damage will be too rapid and death too early for it to occur. Also bear in mind the great efficiency with which llamas and alpacas extract water from their faeces. This is a necessary adaptation to a dry environment, but makes for resistance to the development of diarrhoea as a clinical sign.

Worms are usually borrowed from sheep, and exposure to sheep-grazed pasture is a major risk. Worm burdens build up throughout the summer on ground that is continuously and heavily stocked. If left empty over a hard (i.e. several hard frosts) winter, pasture becomes 'clean'. That is to say, most of the worm larvae die. The pasture becomes reinfested by introducing stock that are carrying worms that have gone dormant inside them; in the spring the larvae reactivate and start producing eggs again.

Your vet can test for worms on dung samples and, if there is evidence of infestation, recommend treatment before your animals become ill. However, not all infestations in the UK produce detectable levels of worm eggs in dung samples. This is thought to be because the worms are not natural parasites of llamas and alpacas, and do not always thrive sufficiently well to breed. Nevertheless, they are still able to do considerable damage to the gut, and animals with low egg counts have shown severe enteric damage on post-mortem examination. Youngstock are particularly at risk.

Whether, when and with what you should treat worms depends on your situation. If an animal has been diagnosed sick with worms, obviously it should be treated. Treatment is usually with an avermectin, e.g. Dectomax, Ivomec, but some species are not killed by these drugs and, when identified, will need treating with (probably) one of the 'white' (benzimidazole) drenches.

If dung samples prove positive for worm eggs treatment may be indicated: it is more common to need to treat youngstock, and just before the onset of winter if dung samples have been positive for worms in the summer. There is usually a seasonal peak of infective worm larvae on the pasture in the middle of summer, during June, July and August, depending on the weather. A dry warm spell followed by rain can result in a rapid rise in parasite larval activity, causing large infestations in animals grazing the ground.

Liver Fluke
This is a flat worm that affects the liver, causing either rapid catastrophic damage, or, more commonly in alpacas, long-term chronic damage. The animals will lose weight, and look generally unthrifty. They may have diarrhoea and may produce fluke eggs in the faeces, but sometimes they simply become dull, fail to stand if approached, and stop eating. Generally local inquiry will reveal that the land supports the snail that is the essential intermediate host for this parasite. Usually this snail can survive only on boggy, wet ground that fails to dry out completely in summer. However, it is always possible for the snails either to move into new territory via a stream, or for the parasite to be imported in other stock (sheep or cattle) and to infest previously 'clean' snails. This will produce a new outbreak of disease in an area previously unaffected. Problems are most often seen from September to November, but seasonality always depends upon the particular weather conditions. Treatment is with e.g. Fasinex (triclabendazole) or albendazole, but be careful with pregnant animals, since albendazole has been associated with birth defects in other species.

Coccidia
This parasite can cause diarrhoea in very young stock, usually as a result of concentrated use of an area or building for calving. It is treatable with e.g. sulfadimidine (Bimadine, if currently available) or diclazuril (Vecoxan). Diarrhoea is not always seen; sometimes an animal is just obviously ill. There are many species of *Coccidia*, and not all are detected by standard methods on dung samples. One particular cause of problems in camelids, *Eimeria macusaniensis*, has such large oocysts (eggs) that they must be looked for with the method usually used for liver fluke.

Cryptosporidia
This parasite causes diarrhoea in very young stock in a similar way to *Coccidia*, but it is more difficult to treat. Prevention is by avoiding contamination and overuse of calving areas.

Lungworm
In cattle and horses, lungworm can be a problem in pasture animals, but it has not so far been diagnosed in llamas and alpacas in the UK. However, the lungworm species that is seen in camelids in South America seems to be much like that in cattle, so the possibility of our animals becoming infested by contact with cattle does exist, at least in theory.

Mites
These parasites are external, affecting the skin. One of the most common of these causes mange, which is described in the section on skin diseases (*see* page 199).

Fly Strike
Fly strike – the presence of flesh-eating maggots on the surface of the body – is rare in alpacas and llamas. Ill or debilitated animals may allow the adult flies to settle and to lay eggs, which hatch into maggots, but only a few cases have been reported. One of these

involved fleece matted with urine and faeces under the tail because of a thorny stick caught in the fleece. In normal circumstances, the grooming habits of these animals seem to protect them from fly strike. Treatment would be as for sheep: trimming the fleece and cleaning the affectted area, antibiotics for infection and insecticide treatment to prevent further attack.

LUNG DISEASES

Perhaps because they are usually kept outside, llamas and alpacas do not seem often to suffer from lung disease. I have treated acute bacterial pneumonia in young animals very occasionally (successfully resolved with antibiotics) but it does not seem to be a common problem.

Tuberculosis

This text was updated in August 2009. The situation regarding tuberculosis in camelids is rather fluid, and the reader should ensure he has up-to-date information regarding current regulations and Government advice.

Alpacas and llamas are susceptible to tuberculosis (TB), and because this disease is a zoonosis, i.e. communicable to man, this susceptibility has a significance far beyond its health implications for the animals themselves.

Affected animals usually show wasting, with respiratory signs like heavy breathing and coughing, terminally. The time taken for visible disease to develop from infection may vary from weeks to years, and sometimes severely affected animals show no loss of condition, and few other signs except perhaps a slight apparent laziness compared with the others in their group.

The UK government has for many years been engaged in a subsidized programme to eradicate TB in cattle, which formed the major reservoir for infection to humans via raw milk. Pasteurization of milk has meant that cattle are now very rarely implicated in the human disease and the costs of this programme have been very high: nearly £74m in the year 2002–2003, although the incidence of TB in cattle is still rising. As a result the TB strategy is being

reviewed, and there is no doubt t hat theoverall objective will be to shift costs to the agricultural industry and away from Government.

The concern that areas that are currently free of TB may become infected is also keenly felt, and cattle farmers strongly resent the lack of restrictions on the movement of camelids. The means by which further spread may be prevented are still under review and are likely to include extended testing together with badger management.

At present, the disease is notifiable in camelids, and the Government does have the power to close premises where it has been identified until animals are tested. Reactors to the test must be removed and slaughtered, and any remaining animals must undergo two clear tests before animal movements may be resumed. However, if infection is merely suspected, there are currently no legal powers to force camelid keepers to test their stock, or to restrict stock movements in the absence of such tests.

It is very likely that camelids will be involved in some sort of screening programme. This is potentially a good thing for the industry since we are all concerned to promote both the health of our animals and that of the public, but the costs to individual owners whose animals are discovered to be infected may be very high.

The difficulty with the whole screening process is the lack of a really accurate test that indicates infection, leading to the relatively frequent failure of the skin test to detect advanced infection. There has been a study conducted in America to determine how good the skin test is in llamas, involving sixty animals, twenty-four of which were experimentally infected with TB. There is no doubt that the test is useful after about forty days post-infection, but again, not 100 per cent accurate, and cross-reactivity with bird TB was demonstrated.

Recent reports indicate that in the early stages of an outbreak animals can be severely ill and even die with the disease without reacting to the skin test. It has also become apparent that camelid movements, especially for mating, where animals can spend some time on other farms, are associated with the spread of infection.

So for now, watch this space. There is always the possibility of our starting up a voluntary scheme of screening for TB infection as they do in New Zealand, with Government permission. This may be a wise move for those who are buying, or already have, very valuable stock to protect. Of course, there is also the possibility of finding that you have the infection in your animals already.

Although it has been widely believed (but not actually proven) that badgers form a reservoir of TB for cattle, it was only in 2004–2005 that an outbreak of TB in alpacas in Ireland was demonstrated to be exactly the same as the infection in the local badgers, where direct contact with cattle had not been thought to occur. It would seem wise to take strenuous precautions to discourage camelid–badger contact, as well as camelid–cattle contact. The Government will, if asked, provide consultation on the best way to do this on an individual holding. A low, triple-wire electric fence with the central wire being earthed seems to be the most effective so far developed.

One final point: the major means of spreading the disease in man is inhaling the infection from the breath of an infected animal or person, so if you like to touch noses with your animals, you need to be confident that they are TB-free.

NEUROLOGICAL DISEASE

This term refers to diseases caused by failure in function of the nervous system, including the brain. There are many possible causes, including bacterial, fungal and viral infections, mineral deficiency, toxicity (poisoning), cancer and metabolic (body chemistry) conditions such as. diabetes and kidney or liver failure.

Hypomagnesaemia
There has been a report of tremors and hyperaesthesia (overreaction to stimuli, producing jerky responses) due to a low level of magnesium in the bloodstream.

Anaemia
This is defined as a lack of iron in the blood, and can mean not enough red cells or not enough iron in each one. It is reported fairly commonly in alpacas an llamas, and usually appears to be of nutritional origin. Iron, copper and cobalt deficiency can all cause an anaemia, as could gut parasitism (worms). The possibility of all of these common causes for anaemia should be assessed. Signs of anaemia are: lying down most of the time; reluctance to run; and tiring easily on exercise. If the gums or vulval mucosa are inspected they will be chalky white (unless pigmented). Sometimes the animal will be observed to eat dirt.

Enterotoxaemia
Enterotoxaemia is an acute disease causing enteritis and sometimes dysentery or death. It is seen in the UK in young cattle, where it is caused by strains of *Clostridium welchii*. Dr Julio Sumar has shown that llamas and alpacas in Peru contract the disease, but that in these cases the strains derive from *Clostridium perfringens*, not *C. welchii*. This is of interest because the Peruvian strains affecting camelids are not contained in Lambivac or Heptavac (vaccines used in sheep and most commonly employed in llamas and alpacas in the UK). Control is achieved by moving calving areas to clean ground.

CONGENITAL DEFECTS

Atresia ani is seen in newborn alpacas. This is where the anus fails to form properly, and there is no hole for faeces to exit. If there is only a thin membrane, it can be treated surgically, but if a longer section of the gut is missing then the cria must be put to sleep. Other deformities of the perineum, including anal stricture (narrowing of the exit hole for the anus), and deformed vaginal opening, plus hermaphroditism, have also been reported.

The likelihood of these deformities having an inherited origin should always be remembered when planning future matings.

FOOT DISEASES

The most common condition of feet is the overgrowth of nails. They vary greatly in how often they need to be trimmed, and this chore is frequently neglected. When they are too long they twist sideways and place strain on toe joints, sometimes distorting them permanently. Once this has happened the animal can never be truly sound again because the toes will not flex and extend normally during locomotion. Toenails can also snap off, exposing the sensitive tissues of the toe – a little like having a fingernail ripped off. (*See* Chapter 5.)

Infectious Pododermatitis (Foot Rot)

This is an infection of the tissues of the foot by bacteria that live in the soil. The affected feet will have swelling, oozing, inflammation and a foul smell, and usually the main area affected is the gap between the toes (known as the interdigital area). The animal will usually be lame, although it seems possible for them to tolerate quite a degree of infection and damage in feet and the inter digital cleft without showing lameness. It should be treated by cleaning the foot thoroughly and applying disinfectants locally (e.g. povidone iodine, chlorhexidine). A foot-bath solution of lincomycin and spectinomycin (Lincospectin) has been used as a daily topical spray successfully. In that instance it was important to blow-dry the feet after treatment, so that the animal could not lick too much drug off. Systemic (injected) antibiotic may be effective.

Prevention is by trying to avoid damage to feet which allow the bacteria into the tissues.

LAMENESS

Check feet first. If the toenails, pads and cleft between the toes are all normal, gently feel up the lame leg, looking for swelling, tenderness or heat. Compare with the sound side, to make sure that anything you spot is genuinely abnormal. Minor injuries will heal with rest, but more severe ones will require veterinary attention. A slight lameness should be monitored and attention sought if it worsens.

Lameness is not a common problem in llamas and alpacas kept in an ideal environment, so recurrent cases should prompt you to look for a cause in your fields or yards, and to consider the Vitamin D status of the animal.

Arthritis

Crias with navel infections could get a bacterial, septic arthritis early in life. Attention to navel hygiene at birth should prevent this. Permanent damage to the joint will result if treatment is not prompt and effective.

An old (especially if obese or previously injured) animal may develop arthritic degenerative joint disease. This will usually manifest as a gradual-onset, worsening lameness.

General stiffness and reluctance to move are seen with certain deficiencies, notably Vitamin D deficiency and selenium deficiency. Anaemia will cause an animal to lie down a lot, and reluctance to stand can be confused with lameness.

SKIN DISEASES

These are common in llamas and alpacas although, unlike many other domestic species, it is rare for a whole group to be severely affected. The typical signs are itchiness, loss of hair and fleece, scabs, and thickening of the skin. The skin usually responds in the same way no matter what the cause of the disease, so the precise signs shown by the animal are not very helpful in determining the cause.

Mange

There are three types of mange mite that can infest llamas and alpacas. These are *Sarcoptes*, *Psoroptes*, and *Chorioptes*. So far in the UK *Sarcoptes* does not seem to have occurred in camelids, and it is speculated that it has been eradicated by the rigorous regimes of parasite treatment in quarantine. *Psoroptes ovis* is the sheep scab mite, and although mites are generally host specific there is some possibility that infestation could

Crusty, bare, scaly ears – a tell-tale sign of skin disease. (Photo: Aiden Foster)

occur from sheep; at the time of writing there had been a single confirmed instance of this mite in two animals. The origin of the infestation was not determined.

Surveys done in the southwest of England by Bristol University seemed to indicate widespread infestation with a particular type of mange mite, *Chorioptes*. The mite was frequently found on animals that did not show signs of disease, as well as those with hair loss, scabs, crusting, skin thickening and itching. This finding led the researcher, Gian Lorenzo d'Alterio, to propose that the presence of disease represented the development of hypersen-

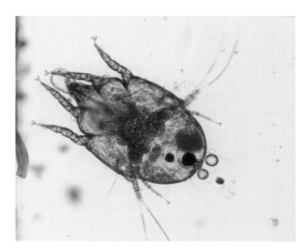

Chorioptes mite under the microscope. They are runners, so you need to be quick to trap them in liquid paraffin when collecting them. (Photo: Aiden Foster)

sitivity in the affected individuals, producing a syndrome rather like sweet-itch in horses, or flea-allergic dermatitis in dogs and cats.

Treatment

Various insecticidal treatments have been attempted, from organo-phosphate sheep sprays, through flea preparations to systemic parasiticides. All seem to have had some effect in some cases and none seem always to work. The commonest current treatment is a group of chemicals called avermectins, usually either the injectable Dectomax (active principle doramectin), or the pour-on Eprinex (eprinomectin). These have the advantage of being persistent in the animal, which obviates the necessity for repeated treatments over a short interval.

The mite can survive for some time off the animal in ideal (warm, moist) conditions, so repeated treatments, treatment of the whole group and quarantine of newly introduced animals all play a part in controlling the condition.

Zinc-Responsive Dermatosis

This has been reported in llamas and alpacas. The signs tend to be the same: crusting, scaling and loss of fleece. Usually itchiness is not a feature, and the fact that these animals have improved after being given zinc supplementation has led to the naming of it as a particular condition. Experts point out that a true deficiency in zinc would produce a wide range of signs, including ill thrift, malaise and infertility, and that the skin signs would be the least of the animal's worries, so it is unlikely that the diet is really deficient in zinc, more that this particular animal needs more for some reason. Some individuals are poorer at absorbing or using particular nutrients, and therefore need more than a normal animal.

It is worth noting here that in some cases of clinical mange where mites have been demonstrated, the affected animals have demonstrably low blood levels of zinc, leading to the speculation that low zinc levels will predispose an individual to clinical mange.

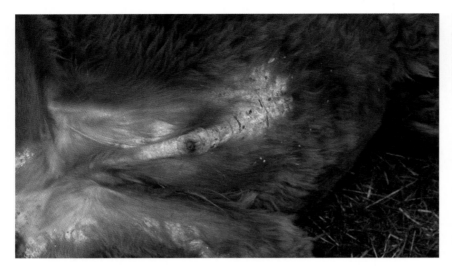

This is the typical appearance of the belly and between the legs of an animal with long-term skin disease. (Photo: Aiden Foster)

Orf

Orf, or Contagious Pustular Dermatitis, has been recorded in alpacas in the UK. It is presumably caught from contact with sheep, in which it is frequently endemic. Its common name in sheep is 'scabby mouth', which describes its signs fairly well. It can affect humans (and is therefore termed a zoonosis). There is no treatment apart from trying to prevent secondary bacterial infection of the crusts where they are severe. It is caught from direct contact with the virus-laden crusts.

Ringworm

This is not a worm at all but a fungal skin infection. It is called ringworm because it sometimes creates circular lesions where the fungus spreads into new healthy skin in a radial fashion. Usually it is not very itchy, but hair loss, flakiness and thickening of the skin occur.

WHEN TO WORRY

The following list of signs should signal to you that something may be amiss:

- Standing or lying around alone.
- Lying on chest with legs out to side instead of normally, in kushed position.
- Abnormally failing to rise when approached.
- Other behavioural changes from normal.
- Not eating.
- Weight loss.
- Not chewing the cud.
- Diarrhoea.
- Colic.
- Straining/apparent constipation.
- Coughing/laboured breathing.
- Discharge from eyes.
- Discharge from nose.
- Discharge from mouth.
- Lameness.
- Skin lesions.
- Itching.
- Collapse.
- Staggering, tremors, nervous twitching or other nervous signs.
- Asymmetrical lumps or bumps.
- Abnormal smell or discharge from any area.

Any of these signs should be investigated. If you cannot satisfy yourself as to the cause of them, and have a plan in place to cure them, you need to call your vet or a knowledgeable friend who can advise you. Remember that these animals are adept at appearing well until seriously ill, so monitoring of subtle changes in behaviour is the only hope of early warning of problems.

Glossary

AFD Average fibre diameter. One of the measurements presented in fibre analysis statistics, which is the mean diameter of the fibres measured in the sample received by the lab. (To get the mean, all of the diameters are added together and then divided by the number of fibres measured.)

anthelmintic A drug that kills internal parasitic worms (helminths).

atresia ani Failure of the anus to develop in the foetus, resulting in a cria that cannot pass faeces.

blanket The area over the back and sides of an alpaca, where the finest fleece is to be found.

blowing out The term used to describe the tendency of fleeces to become coarser as the animal gets older. In some animals the effect is quite dramatic, and can cause the fleeces from animals older than about three years to be commercially worthless. In all animals it is expected that the first fleece will be the finest, but the ability to retain most of the fineness into maturity is enormously valuable and, crucially, inherited.

bonnet The topknot of fleece on an alpaca's forehead.

breeding value The value assigned to an individual animal with respect to a particular physical characteristic, which indicates the likelihood of that animal's passing the characteristic on to its offspring.

C1 Compartment one, the first and largest compartment of the stomach system of llamas and alpacas. The others are termed C2 and C3.

camelids Animals descended from a common camel-like ancestor, including llamas, alpacas, guanacos, vicuna, Arabian camels, and bactrian camels. Used in this book to refer collectively to the South American camelids: llamas, alpacas, guanaco, and vicuna.

cleansing Another term for the placenta, or afterbirth – the membrane passed after calving.

colic Abdominal pain and its associated signs.

corpus luteum The structure in the ovary that is formed from the follicle after ovulation. It produces progesterone to assist in the establishment of a pregnancy.

coverage The degree to which an alpaca has dense fleece down its legs, often providing a guide to the weight of premium fibre it will yield at shearing.

cria Spanish word for baby, and used to refer to llamas, alpacas, guanaco and vicuna in the first few months of life.

crimp The uniform, wavy, corrugated look of a parted alpaca fleece, and one of the characteristics assessed in determination of fleece quality.

CV (Coefficient of Variation) One of the measurements presented in fibre analysis statistics. This expresses the standard deviation as a percentage of the average (mean) fibre diameter. It gives a guide to the uniformity of the fibre diameters throughout the sample; it is desirable to have a CV that is lower than the AFD and in any case, as low as possible.

dry matter Food with all the water evaporated, an idea used to compare nutrient content and feed intake of different feeds.

dystocia Obstructed birth.

genotype The genetic make-up of the animal. This includes any genes that are carried but not expressed in the animal, and that may be passed on to the offspring. *See also* phenotype.

guard hair The thick, straight, longer, prickly hair which overlies the softer undercoat. If processed with the undercoat, it produces a prickly feeling to the fabric. See also medullation.

helminths Internal parasitic worms.

hembra Spanish for female, sometimes used to refer to a female alpaca or llama.

histogram The bar graph commonly used to display the information about the microscopic measurements of fleece.

huacaya The woolly-looking type of alpaca whose fleece stands up like a sheep fleece. (pronounced *wa-kai-yah*). (*See* suri.)

huarizo The South American term for a cross between a llama and an alpaca (pronounced *wa-ree-tho*).

imprinting The process of a newborn animal developing a set of sensory signals for recognizing its mother. This word is used to refer to hand-reared animals that have been imprinted by humans in place of their mothers.

interdigital cleft The space between the toes.

liquid paraffin A clear mineral oil used most often as a laxative because it is not digested or absorbed when taken by mouth. Not to be confused with fuel oil!

luteinization The process by which a follicle switches from producing oestrogen to producing progesterone, usually because ovulation has occurred.

macho Spanish for male, sometimes used to refer to a male alpaca or llama.

medullation The presence of hollow, air-filled fibres, which are much thicker, and therefore prickly to the touch, in the fleece. This term is also used to refer to the presence of guard hair in a fleece, although strictly speaking guard hairs and medullated fibres are not exactly the same thing.

micron One thousandth of a milimetre (i.e. one millionth of a metre). The unit used to measure the diameter of fibres.

micron count The average (mean) fibre diameter expressed in microns. It is used to denote fineness of a fleece.

molassed Describes feed that has had molasses (unrefined sugar syrup) added to it. It makes the feed sweet and palatable, and raises the energy content.

oesophagus Also sometimes called the gullet, this is the tube that carries food and drink from the mouth to the stomach.

oestrogen The female hormone, produced by maturing egg follicles, which causes sexually receptive behaviour.

orgling, orgle The particular guttural call made by the male alpaca or llama at mating.

perineum The area around the anus, under the tail.

peristalsis The squeezing, massaging movements of the digestive tract to move its contents along its length.

phenotype The physical make-up of the animal, which is a result of the expression of some of its genetic material. Phenotype is the measurable, observable form. *See also* genotype.

primary fibre A thick, strong, hairy fibre growing in skin. Primary fibres are each surrounded by a population of much finer secondary fibres. Fine fleece animals are selectively bred to have as low a ratio of primary to secondary fibres as possible, because the primary fibres cause prickle in a finished garment.

progeny testing The collection and comparison of data on the offspring of breeding animals (usually males, because they can have more offspring) to test the degree to which the parent animal is able to pass on particular characteristics.

progesterone The female hormone mainly responsible for causing the changes in the body required to maintain a pregnancy.

rejection Alternative term for 'spitting off'; a

rejection by a female of a male's attempts to mate.

SAC South American Camelid.

second cuts Very short bits of fleece, which are produced when the shears accidentally rise away from the skin during shearing, leaving too much fleece still on the animal. The shearer takes a 'second cut' to remove the rest of the fleece, but the resulting fragments of fleece are useless to processors because they are too short. They should be skirted and shaken off before the fleece goes for processing.

seconds An abreviation for second quality fleece, which must be separated from the blanket at shearing. Usually from the belly, legs, tail, head and parts of the neck.

SD (standard deviation) One of the measurements presented in fibre analysis statistics. This measures the variability in the sample. For example, in a sample where there is a very great difference between the finest and the coarsest fibres, the standard deviation would be high. Since uniformity of the fibres is desirable, low standard deviations are best.

skirting The process of separating the best fleece from that of second and third quality, and of removing contaminated fleece, in preparation for classing and processing.

spitting off This is the term for rejection of the male's advances by a female, and also for the process of teasing the female to see whether she is receptive. (*See* teasing.)

staple The block or bundle into which huacaya fleece separates when parted.

staple definition The clarity with which the blocky bundles can be seen separating from each other when the fleece is parted.

staple length The length of the fibre from skin to tip.

strong fibre A polite term for coarser fibre.

suri The term used to describe alpacas whose fleece hangs down in long ringlet-like locks. The suri gene is dominant, so even half-huacaya animals will display the suri fleece pattern.

teasing The practice of putting a male and female animal together to see whether the female is sexually receptive. In the case of llamas and alpacas, a receptive female will 'sit', i.e. adopt the kush position, when she is willing to mate.

tenderness The expression for weak fibre. Usually this is the result of the animal having been ill at some point, causing a period of restricted fibre growth, during which the individual fibres became weakened. This part of the fibre then breaks easily, making it problematic to process.

tenesmus Persistent straining as if to urinate or defecate.

topical A treatment applied to the outside surface of the patient, e.g. sprays, creams, lotions.

trace elements Minerals that are only required in at a very low level in the diet, even though they are absolutely necessary.

uniformity The presence of a consistent level of quality and colour throughout all of the areas of fleece on an animal's body – especially important in the blanket area. Once shorn from the animal, it is important that a lot submitted for processing is uniform throughout.

vulva The outer lips of the vagina.

wool blind Describes an animal with so much fleece around the eyes that it cannot see.

zoonosis Any disease in animals that can be contracted by humans.

Further Reading and References

Alpaca World (periodical), *see* Useful Addresses.

Anderson, David E. DVM, MS, Diplomate AVCS. Proceedings BVCS Conference 2003.

Birutta, Gail, *Storey's Guide to Raising Llamas*, Storey Books, USA (2000).

Cebra, Chris, DVM. Proceedings BVCS Conference 2004.

Daugherty, Stanlynn, *Packing with Llamas*, Juniper Ridge Press, USA (1994).

Fowler, Murray E. DVM, *Medicine and Surgery of South American Camelids: Llama, Alpaca, Vicuna, Guanaco*, Iowa State University Press, USA (1997).

Harmon, David and Rubin, Amy S., *Llamas on the Trail: A Packer's Guide*, Mountain Press (1998).

Hoffman, Clare, and Asmus, J., *Caring for Llamas and Alpacas: A Health and Management Guide*, Rocky Mountain Llama Association, USA (2000).

Hoffman, Eric, *The Complete Alpaca*. (For further information on international screening, refer to Eric Hoffman's original work for the Alpaca Registry Inc.)

Hoffman, Eric, and Fowler, Murray E. DVM, *The Alpaca Book*, Clay Press Inc. (1995).

Mallon, John *Halter Training Basics* (video).

McGee, Marty, *The Camelid Companion*. Also numerous publications and videos.

Tellington Jones, Linda, *The Tellington Touch: A Breakthrough Technique to Train and Care for Your Favourite Animal*, Viking (1992).

Vaughan, Jane, *Alpaca World*, Winter 2004/5.

Useful Addresses

EQUIPMENT SUPPLIERS

Quality Llama Products Inc.
33217 Bellinger Scale Road
Lebanon
Oregon 97355
USA

UK Llamas (UK agents for Quality Llama
    Products.)
New House Farm
Mosterton
Beaminster
Dorset
DT8 3HE
Tel: 01308 868674

Camelidynamics (Marty McGee Bennett's
    range of equipment)
Julie Taylor-Browne
Carthvean Alpacas
Tel: 01209 831672

M. R. Harness
Kingswood Hollow
Stanford Road
Great Witley
Worcestershire
WR6 6JG
Tel: 01299 896827

MINI-MILLS

Alan Glover and Iona Humphries
Alborada Alpacas
Lower Claydon Hill Farm
Steeple Claydon
Buckingham
MK18 2EN
Tel: 01296 730040
email: Alborada@btinternet.com
www.thetreestump.co.uk/temp/index.htm

Mike and Celia Berry
NorWEFT
Tel: 01352 720382
email: berryenterprising@supanet.com

Trevor Stables and Dick Darlington
Farrlacey Alpacas
Horncastle
Lincolnshire
Tel: 01507 568249
email: farrlacey@aol.com
www.farrlacey.co.uk

Meon Valley Mill
Tel: 01489 878833
email: enquiries@meonvalleymill.co.uk
www.meonvalleymill.co.uk

Other Processing Mills

UK Alpaca Ltd
Vulscombe Farm
Pennymoor
Tiverton
Devon
EX16 8NB
Tel: 01598 753644
email: info@ukalpaca.com
    ukalpaca@jarbon.com
www.ukalpaca@jarbon.com

Specialist Spinning Ltd
Cotefield Farm
Bodicote
Banbury
Oxon
OX15 4AQ
Tel: 01295 811766

FIBRE AND YARN SHOPS

Jarbon Textiles
PO Box 8
Lynton
Devon
EX35 6WY
Tel: 01598 752490
email: info@jarbon.com
www.jarbon.com

Coldharbour Mill
Uffculme
Cullompton
Devon
EX15 3EE
Tel: 01884 840960
email: info@coldharbourmill.org.uk
www.coldharbourmill.org.uk
(Specializes in alpaca, British wool, merino and silk.)

FEEDS

Charnwood Feeds
Framlingham
Suffolk
Tel: 01728 622 300

Camelid Complete Feeds
Tel: 0845 6076559
www.alpaca-nutrition.co.uk

Newline Feeds
Newline Link 01684 294945

SOCIETIES

British Veterinary Camelid Society
Foxes Grove
Punnetts Town
Heathfield
East Sussex
TN21 9PE
email: secretary@camelidvets.org
www.camelidvets.org

The BVCS is a society of veterinary surgeons who have an interest in camelids, and who run an annual conference and maintain a website and chatroom in order to keep up with latest developments in camelid medicine.

The British Alpaca Society
c/o Grassroots Systems Ltd
P.O. Box 251
Exeter
EX2 8WX
Tel: 0845 3312468
email: info@bas-uk.com
www.bas-uk.com

MAGAZINE

Alpaca World
Vulscombe Farm
Cruwys Morchard
Tiverton
Devon
EX16 8NB

Index